Concise Version of

APPALACHIA
Social Context Past and Present
Fifth Edition
Edited by Phillip J. Obermiller and Michael E. Maloney

For Steven Parkansky
Morehead State University

This publication is a concise version of *Appalachia: Social Context Past and Present, Fifth Edition,* edited by Phillip J. Obermiller and Michael E. Maloney.

Kendall Hunt
publishing company

www.kendallhunt.com
Send all inquiries to:
4050 Westmark Drive
Dubuque, IA 52004-1840

Copyright © 2011 by Kendall Hunt Publishing Company

ISBN 978-0-7575-9015-3

All rights reserved. No part of this publication may be reproduced, stored in a retrieval system, or transmitted, in any form or by any means, electronic, mechanical, photocopying, recording, or otherwise, without the prior written permission of the copyright owner.

Printed in the United States of America
10 9 8 7 6 5 4 3 2 1

Contents

Chapter 1   1. "Appalachia" 1
             by Richard A. Couto

Chapter 2   2. "The Sociology of Southern Appalachia" 13
             by David S. Walls and Dwight B. Billings

Chapter 3   13. "Beyond Isolation and Homogeneity: Diversity and the History of Appalachia" 23
             by Ronald L. Lewis

Chapter 4   20. "Work, Poverty, and Health in Appalachia" 37
             by Richard A. Couto, Phillip J. Obermiller, and Julia C. DeBruicker

Chapter 5   22. "Rape of the Appalachians" 43
             by Jedediah S. Purdy

Chapter 6   27. "The Mountain Crafts: Romancing the Marketplace" 51
             by Garry Barker

Chapter 7   25. "From Farm to Coal Camp to Back Office and McDonald's: Living in the Midst of Appalachia's Latest Transformation" 55
             by Sally Ward Maggard

Chapter 8   33. "The Grass Roots Speak Back" 67
             by Stephen L. Fisher

CHAPTER 1

Appalachia

by Richard A. Couto

The Appalachian region has had many different boundaries. Currently, the Appalachian Regional Commission (ARC) uses a specific geopolitical definition of 410 counties in 13 states. Previously, social scientists used several different sets of boundaries to delineate the region. In addition to geographic boundaries, Appalachia denotes a distinct cultural region of contradictory and incorrect popular conceptions focusing on quilts, dulcimers, and images of universal poverty and hardship. All these elements of the popular conception of the region can be found in Appalachia; none of them describes the entire region or all the people who live there. These cultural images offer conflicting interpretations of the region but only a small sense of the diversity to be found there. It is difficult to make a safe generalization about the Appalachian region. This chapter offers an overview of the region that explains why generalizations are difficult. It examines geographic and cultural boundaries of Appalachia and offers an analytical framework to understand cultural representations of the region.

DEFINING THE GEOGRAPHIC REGIONS

Different researchers have used various geographic boundaries for the region. Early sociologists, like Campbell (1921) and Kephart (1913), established boundaries, such as the southern highlands, that united a group of people with some common cultural characteristics. Kephart's study incorporated an uncertain number of counties in the Great Smoky Mountains region of North Carolina, Georgia, and Tennessee. Campbell's study offered a much broader definition—210 counties in 9 states extending north of Kephart's region. A 1960 study by the Maryland Department of Economic Development expanded the boundaries of the region to 11 states from New York to Alabama (Ford 1962). A survey conducted by Ford (1962) included 205 counties in just 6 states. By the mid-1960s, a half-century of analysis had provided several different geographic boundaries for Appalachia.

In 1965, the Appalachian Regional Development Act, which created the Appalachian Regional Commission, drew the boundaries of

Source: From *Sowing Seeds in the Mountains: Community-Based Conditions for Cancer Prevention and Control* by Richard Couto, Nancy Simpson & Gale Harris. NIH Publication #94-3779, National Cancer Institute, 1994. Data updated 2006 for the fifth edition.

the region once again. These boundaries, the most expansive to date, have become widely accepted. They follow the spine of the Appalachian Mountains from the southern tier of New York counties to a tier of northeast Mississippi counties. The region encompasses 410 counties and 13 states, including all of West Virginia and portions of Alabama, Georgia, Kentucky, Maryland, Mississippi, New York, North Carolina, Ohio, Pennsylvania, South Carolina, Tennessee, and Virginia.

The current definition, like that of ARC, came from a national sense of acute human need within a region and a national commitment to do something about it. It also resulted from an effort of state and congressional leaders to include their jurisdictions in an area of special federal initiatives. Federal administrators welcomed this initiative. They built much congressional support for the Appalachian Regional Commission, a fledgling agency of the Kennedy administration, which was a precursor of "War on Poverty" programs in the 1960s. Geography interacted with centers of power in Washington, D.C., to push the region's boundaries farther and farther. Initially, the ARC region included only 11 states. New York was added because it was contiguous. Mississippi was added also because it was contiguous and contained two senior U.S. senators who could be powerful friends to a federal program (Raitz and Ulack 1984). The region continued to change at its edges, gaining six counties since 1991.

Thus, the Appalachian Mountains are only part of the logic of this broad geographic definition. Other parts of that logic include economic similarities, contiguity, measures of low income and human well-being, and congressional representation of 26 senators and 59 members of the House of Representatives. That logic continues with some changes. Some Appalachian states lost congressional representation (e.g., New York), and others gained (e.g., Georgia). More than 40 years of programs and reports create additional reasons to accept ARC's geographic boundaries. In addition, local political and business elites in 410 counties are now organized into economic development areas and provide local support, giving the region an additional unique feature. In some ways, this geographic definition continues former definitions but adds specific political and administrative criteria.

Nearly all geographic definitions of Appalachia encompass an area with diverse economies and populations that make generalizations difficult. ARC's definition compounds this difficulty. It includes areas that forged the heart of the Industrial Revolution with steel and coal. Areas of the region demonstrated the possibility of mass production of goods and textiles and pioneered in the development of chemicals and plastics. Other parts of Appalachia with economic bases of agriculture and tourism remain only indirectly touched by the Industrial Revolution. This part of the region includes numerous rural counties with populations of less than 10,000. On the other hand, the region includes Pittsburgh and Birmingham and is contiguous to other major metropolitan areas including Atlanta, Cincinnati, Harrisburg, Lexington, Memphis, and Montgomery. Other major cities, including Albany, Baltimore, Buffalo, Cleveland, Columbus, Nashville, New York, Philadelphia, and Washington, D.C., are within an hour's drive of ARC's Appalachian boundaries.

Analysts concede the diversity within the Appalachian region by use of subregions: Northern, Central, and Southern Appalachia. The northern subregion takes in most of the older industrial area of the region and the nation, including all the Appalachian counties in Maryland, New York, Ohio, and Pennsylvania. In addition, counties in Virginia and West Virginia are included in Northern Appalachia. Central Appalachia, the smallest of the subregions, includes all the counties of eastern Kentucky and some of the Appalachian counties of Tennessee, Virginia, and West Virginia. Southern Appalachia includes the remainder of Appalachian counties of Tennessee and Virginia as well as all the Appalachian counties of Alabama, Georgia, Mississippi, North Carolina,

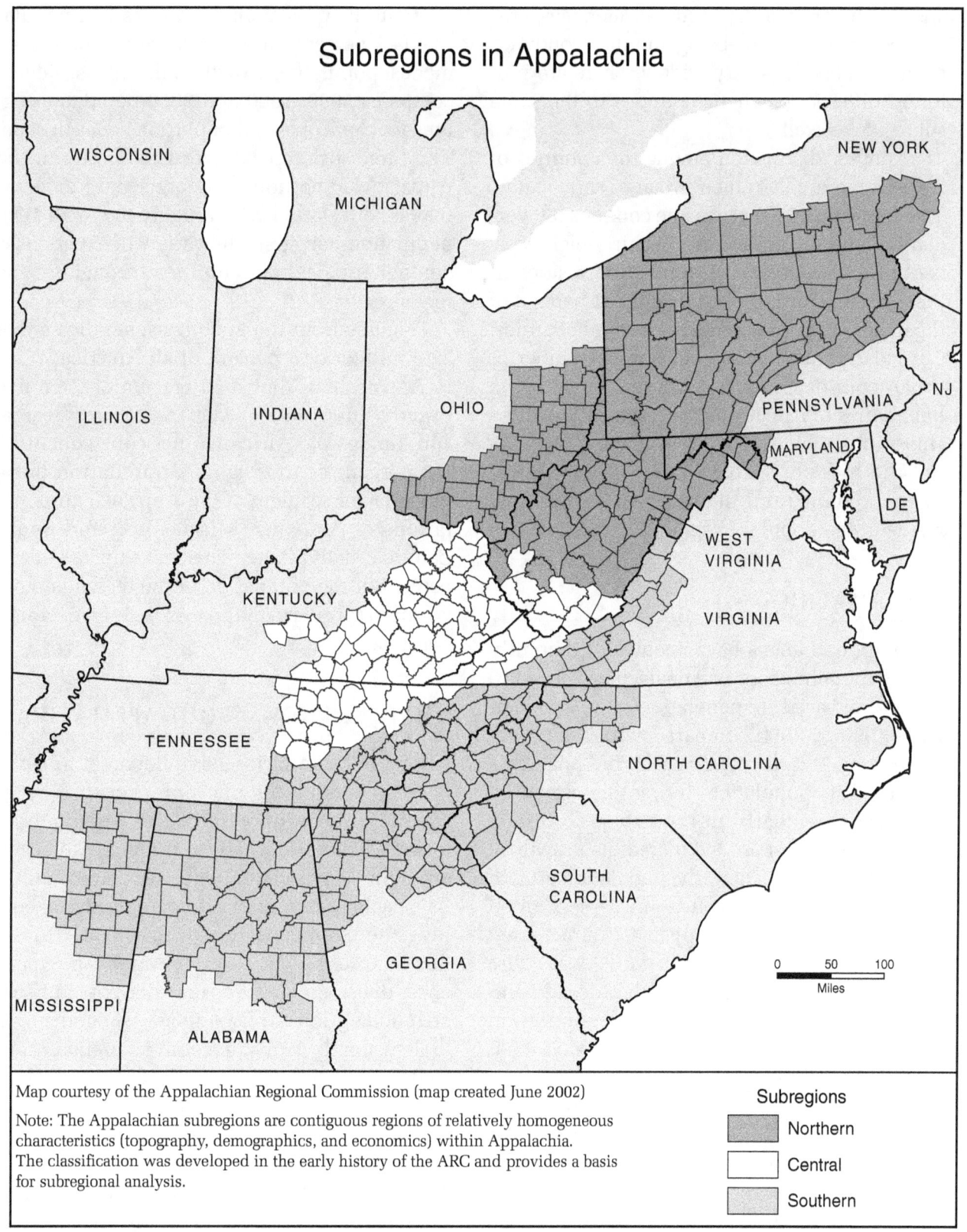

Figure 1 The Appalachian Region

and South Carolina. As discussed later, measures of socioeconomic well-being and the economies of these subregions vary widely. There are profound differences among counties in the same subregion as well.

Another distinction among the counties of Appalachia involves their urban or rural status. Two hundred and seventy-one counties (66 percent) of the region are rural. Thirty-eight percent of the Appalachian population resides in these rural counties, whereas only 21 percent of the total U.S. population lives in rural counties. Central Appalachia has the fewest number of urban counties. Figure 1 offers a view of the boundaries of Appalachia, and sets off the three subregions. Obviously, this geographic region is not the hidden, socioeconomically homogeneous, remote, and distinct region that may reside in the popular imagination.

DEMOGRAPHICS

Population changes have occurred differently among the subregions of Appalachia. The entire region increased its population by 9.1 percent from 1990 to 2000 compared with a national increase of 13.2 percent. Southern Appalachia increased its population during this period by 18 percent—mostly in the urban counties. These figures obscure the incredible growth in suburban Atlanta. There, the population growth of one county—Gwinnett County—accounted for 56 percent of all of Appalachia's increased population between 1980 and 1990. The county's population doubled that decade and the next. From 1990 to 2000, its population growth "slowed" to 60 percent and amounted to almost 600,000 people.

Northern Appalachian counties had a population decline (3.1 percent) from 1980 to 1990, especially among the urban counties of that subregion (3.9 percent). This subregion had modest but positive population growth in the 1990s. Appalachian New York lost population, while Appalachian Pennsylvania barely kept its place as did West Virginia (0.9 percent and 0.8 percent respectively).

Central Appalachian counties lost population (4.7 percent) in the 1980s and experienced modest population growth in the 1990s. Table 1 compares 1980, 1990 and 2000 population figures for the Appalachian portions of each state. The large differences over time between the Appalachian portions of Georgia and Kentucky, which both started with roughly the same 1980 populations, suggests the variety of experiences among Appalachian counties throughout the region.

Figures from the 2000 census indicate that 22.9 million or 8 percent of all Americans live in Appalachia. Almost 50 percent of them live in only three states—Alabama, Pennsylvania, and Tennessee. African Americans constitute 8.2 percent of the region's population but a much larger segment of the Appalachian populations of Alabama, Mississippi, and South Carolina. Native Americans make up less than 1 percent of the population of the region and are concentrated primarily in western North Carolina.

WHAT WE KNOW ABOUT APPALACHIA

After the boundaries have been set and the people counted, the question occurs: What is special and unique about the Appalachian region? Writers, journalists, and video and camera crews have visited specific places within Appalachia's boundaries to explain mistakenly how the characteristics of the people found there express a variation of American experience: dialect, a specific rural lifestyle and subsistence agriculture, godlessness, godliness, violent family feuds, excessive parental affection, industrial work, exploitation of labor, organized resistance of workers to exploitation, or poverty in large amounts and severe forms. Even the early, more focused studies of Appalachia conducted by Kephart (1913) and Campbell (1921) cautioned against generalizations concerning the residents of the region. Campbell explained that the people of Appalachia were socially heterogeneous, despite being white in overwhelming numbers

Table 1 Appalachian Population* by State, 1980, 1990, and 2000

	Population			Percent Change		
Date	1980	1990	2000	1980–2000	1980–1990	1990–2000
Appalachian Part						
Alabama	2,430,244	2,529,623	2,837,224	16.7	4.1	10.4
Georgia	1,103,971	1,508,030	2,207,531	99.9	36.6	42.7
Kentucky	1,077,095	1,045,357	1,141,511	6.0	−2.9	6.6
Maryland	220,132	224,477	236,699	7.5	2.0	5.4
Mississippi	498,374	510,400	615,452	23.4	2.4	8.9
New York	1,083,241	1,088,470	1,072,786	−0.9	0.5	−1.4
North Carolina	1,217,732	1,306,682	1,526,207	25.3	7.3	16.8
Ohio	1,376,130	1,372,893	1,455,313	5.8	−0.2	6.0
Pennsylvania	5,994,240	5,769,410	5,814,800	−2.9	−3.8	0.9
South Carolina	793,040	888,057	1,028,656	29.7	12.0	15.8
Tennessee	2,073,834	2,146,992	2,479,317	19.6	3.5	15.5
Virginia	549,888	517,816	665,177	21.0	−5.8	4.0
West Virginia	1,950,183	1,793,477	1,808,344	−7.3	−8.0	0.8
Appalachia	20,368,104	20,701,684	22,894,014	12.4	1.6	9.1
United States	226,545,805	248,709,873	281,421,906	24.2	9.8	13.2

*Data for 399 Appalachian counties.
Source: Appalachian Regional Commission.

and living in a specifically defined contiguous area. Moreover, he understood that statements about people in the remote rural areas of his study could not be applied with equal accuracy to the people in the same region who lived in towns and valleys (Campbell 1921).

As the boundaries of Appalachia expanded, the differences among people within the region also grew, making generalizations about residents in the region even more difficult. For example, how do residents in Ithaca, New York, and Tupelo, Mississippi, share an Appalachian culture; or residents of Pittsburgh and the Atlanta suburbs; or Binghamton, New York, and Estill County, Kentucky?

Generalizations about the residents of the Appalachian region and their culture come primarily from disregard of cautions about extrapolating from one set of people to another, from one place to another, or from one time to another. Very few studies encompass the entire region and its many issues. Most studies deal with Central Appalachia—eastern Kentucky and contiguous portions of east Tennessee, southwestern Virginia, and southern West Virginia. Other studies are even more limited to a particular community in a particular county in Central or Southern Appalachia.

Caudill's influential book (1962), *Night Comes to the Cumberlands: A Biography of a Depressed Area,* is still a widely read classic and a very good historical introduction. However, it addresses only a portion of the coalmining counties in eastern Kentucky. There are problems extrapolating Caudill's work to other coalmining counties, as well as to the noncoal counties, of eastern Kentucky. Based on Caudill's work, it is simply impossible to generalize, for example, to the anthracite coalfields of Pennsylvania, to the portion of Central Appalachia that is not coal mining, or to the rest of the region as defined by ARC.

Caudill's book mixes two strong but distinct interpretations of the problems of the Central Appalachian region. Caudill blames the social origins and inbreeding of the region's residents for its political, social, and economic problems. In this, he resembles those who have used a culture-of-poverty analysis to explain the region. Weller's (1965) prominent work, *Yesterday's People,* illustrates this approach as do numerous other studies most often written by helping professionals, including mental health workers. Cunningham (1987) has taken up the cultural interpretation most recently in his book—*Apples on the Flood: The Southern Mountain Experience*—although much more adroitly than others and without victim blaming. Caudill's work is so rooted in victim blaming that psychologist Arthur Jensen, in a television interview with journalist William Buckley in the early 1970s, averted charges that his studies of IQ and African Americans were racist by appealing to Caudill's work.

On a more popular front, *The Foxfire Book* (Wigginton 1972) emphasized Appalachian culture in a much more positive manner. These accounts of folklore and folkways portray a self-reliant, talented, and intelligent group of rural people. However, generalizations can no more be made from this work, done primarily in rural, northern Appalachian Georgia, than they can from Caudill's work.

As a result of numerous studies and reports, Appalachia conjures up conflicting and inaccurate images of people who live there. On the one hand, we have television's "The Waltons," offered as a model in the 1992 Republican presidential campaign on family values; on the other hand, we have the Hatfields and the McCoys, commercialized as bumbling bumpkins or fiendishly cruel, like the residents of rural Georgia portrayed in the film Deliverance. Similarly, popular images suggest the cartoon indolence and innocence of Li'l Abner and Snuffy Smith and news coverage of the grueling work and militancy of nameless coal miners.

Scholarly examinations trace the popular concepts of Appalachia and their origins back to national trends in markets for literature and social interventions. Literary magazines seeking short stories of local color found them in descriptions of parts of Appalachia. Social workers in settlement schools found contributions for their work in responses to their descriptions of the needs of the residents of the region whom they served and the many more they did not (Shapiro 1978). Later, political and social activists looking for places that needed change found them in the conditions of poverty in Appalachia as well (Batteau 1990). People outside the Appalachian region often have defined the region in terms of their commercial, financial, social, or political needs. This is not to say there is no accuracy in the accounts that we have. It does suggest an additional reason why the generalizations we have of the Appalachian region may be misguided as well as misinformed.

In addition to his emphasis on the characteristics of the Appalachian people in his study, Caudill (1962) also interpreted the region's problems in terms of corporate control and related political collusion. Others have built on this interpretation to place Appalachian events and conditions into the mainstream of American life and processes of industrialization and economic development. In these studies, Appalachian conditions of poverty and human need are more the consequence of economic decision making by coal companies, textile mills, the timber industry, and absentee landowners. The region's extractive industry sends minerals and timber to wealthier areas and receives as little in return as possible. Legislation to benefit the companies developing the raw materials of the region left local and state governments with little tax base to provide essential services such as education, medical care, and public health. The political corruption that went into forming this legislative inequity left reformers with few avenues to justice (Appalachian Land Ownership Task Force 1983; Eller 1982; Gaventa 1980; Lewis et al. 1978). One study reinterprets the feud of the Hatfields and the McCoys, which has stimulated so many stereotypes of "hillbillies," in terms of the economic transformation going on at the time (Waller 1988).

Unlike the cultural interpretations of Appalachia, these studies emphasize what national economic and political forces have done to the region. Likewise, rather than an interpretation of a culture that incapacitated citizens to resist negative influences, these studies suggest how people fought back against such forces. When taken together, even these studies of the Appalachian region are limited in providing an overview of the region broadly defined by the Appalachian Regional Commission. They also focus on a particular set of counties, once again most often in Central Appalachia; a particular time; or a particular industry (e.g., coal, textiles, steel).

In sum, what we "know" about Appalachia is largely extrapolated from case studies, most often from Central or Southern Appalachia; from historical studies of a set of counties, an industry (e.g., coal), or labor union efforts; and from cultural descriptions and interpretations of very specific places or practices. What we "know" often obscures the fact that Appalachian residents, regardless of subregion, are average and ordinary human beings, who under a given environment will develop like other human beings. Part of the problem of Appalachia is what we "know" about it and have to unlearn. In this regard, Appalachian social problems resemble other social problems such as race (Du Bois 1935, p. iii).

Addressing the social problems of Appalachia, no less than any other region, requires knowledge of the social and historical factors that have shaped those problems and the cultural responses that residents of a particular place have fashioned. If there is a culture of poverty, it is in large part a response to the poverty in which people found themselves living and a reasonable response to their prospects of escaping it. Likewise, if there are cultural traits like fatalism, they are likely, in large measure, to be a response to the lack of resources required to improve a condition.

Much of the historical and social analysis of the region provides only for safe generalizations of particular places at particular times. As with any other region, we have to accept change over time in the same place and differences among places even in the same region. The expanse of the Appalachian region and the conflicting standards used in defining it make these cautions about generalizations essential. We have become especially cautious in making generalizations about Appalachian culture, the topic to which we now turn.

THE CULTURAL REPRESENTATION OF APPALACHIA

Few areas of Appalachia attract more attention today than the area of culture. Caudill's (1962) and Weller's (1965) emphases on unique characteristics such as fatalism remain popular, especially among helping professionals who are new to the region and seek to adapt to the culture. Caudill and Weller offer handy hooks on which it is easy to hang innovative interventions and expressions of concern. Their interpretations allow helping professionals to portray the region as beyond the mainstream waiting to be brought in with the tools of professional intervention.

Work following that of Caudill and Weller explains Appalachian culture in positive terms and the seemingly differentiating negative characteristics as expressions of differentiating economic circumstances. Prominent among these later cultural treatments, Appalshop, a media collective in Whitesburg, Kentucky, tells the virtues of Central Appalachia in film, video, radio broadcast, and theater. Individual Appalachians contributed the major portion of this recent work on the positive cultural traits of Appalachians. Often their studies begin with a narrative account in which they acquire their Appalachian identity only upon contact with institutions, such as colleges, away from their home; this acquisition imparts shame for their origins and their low circumstances; they reclaim their pride in the virtues of their unique, no longer suppressed identity; and they present their current work as one variant of the valuable multicultural American experience (Blair 1993).

In some cases, these authors defiantly assert the superiority of Appalachian ways over others. For example, Grigsby (1993) contrasted his working-class background of the coalmining region of eastern Kentucky with the middle-class, academic culture of which he is now a part as a college teacher. In particular, he recalled his chagrin at the conduct of his departmental chair who expressed anger that Grigsby had not attended a party and had not responded with his intention to come or not to come. That anger was coupled with disbelief and disdain that Grigsby did not know what RSVP means. Grigsby then counterattacked in this conflict of cultures.

> I don't like "RSVP" invitations. I don't like being forced to decide early to attend an event and then be forced to go later if I don't want to, and I'm convinced that the working-class approach to such functions ("Come if you want and can and bring something to eat or drink") is a more logical way to conduct "parties," or to use the working-class word—"get-togethers"—which is again more logical (Grigsby 1993, p. 8).

This form of cultural counterattack comes with deep resentment—"dismay and venom" (Speer 1993, p. 12)—over the continued assumption of inferiority of Appalachian culture. Tracing their intellectual protest back to work of Branscome, Seltzer, Whisnant, and others in the early 1970s, these recent accounts testify to the staying power of pejorative stereotypes of "hillbillies." In 1999 sociologist Dwight Billings, novelist Gurney Norman, and independent scholar Katherine Ledford were outraged by the Broadway success of Robert Schenkkan's Pulitzer award winning play, The Kentucky Cycle. They collected a set of essays to explain once again the practice of stereotyping Appalachians, and the profit some receive by exploiting these images (Billings, Norman, and Ledford, 1999).

Other ethnic groups have exemptions from comic books; for example, one does not find comic books on Hasidic Jews, Mormons, or Latinos. Likewise, it is hard to imagine finding a book on how to speak "eastern" as easily as one finds books on speaking "southern" and "hillbilly." We continue to caricature Appalachia, however, in whole and in part, in comic strips, television shows and reruns, movies, and even in countless souvenir shops at interstate exits throughout the region.

It is simply inconceivable that after the civil rights movement we would base our understanding of African Americans on blackface comedy, such as television reruns of "Amos and Andy." Social and political change has come with cultural changes regarding race. This has spilled over into other areas such as gender. Thus a "Women's Joke Book" would be funny to more people if it contained jokes told by women instead of jokes told by men about women. These changes contrast sharply with the unchanged status of Appalachian cultural stereotypes (Crawford 1993). In the mid-1980s, John Shelton Reed affirmed the continuation of what others had pointed out in the early 1970s: "Hillbillies appear to be the last acceptable ethnic fools" (Speer 1993, p. 18).

These observations illustrate a much larger background of cultural representation that has been addressed by other writers. For example, Batteau assumes that stereotypes are images made in the context of intergroup relationships in which "different groups seek to impose their will on others" (Batteau 1990, p. 199). Similarly, Whisnant (1983, p. 6) relates Appalachian cultural representation to the politics of culture. In the latter, misleading concepts of local people are disseminated to people with influence and wealth as part of the interaction of very different cultural systems. The distant cultural systems (e.g., centers of industrial capital in the United States in the late 19th century) focus on parts of the local culture. By separating parts of local culture from the broader social, political, and economic history that explains local culture, the distant cultural systems obscure the political implications of their own efforts to change local culture (Whisnant 1983,

p. 16). In doing so, these distant cultural systems assume the superiority of their own cultural forms and establish the justification for their efforts at change.

Cunningham (1987) places Whisnant's work in an intermediary range of cultural conflict. Cunningham views culture, politics, and economics as a seamless web woven from the interactions of three groups: the metropolitan core region or civilized group, the outside region or savage group, and the intermediate region that lies between the two other groups. He applies his analytical framework to the interaction of Rome (civilized, metropolitan core), the Celts and Scottish highlanders (the savage outside region), and the Scottish lowlanders and Ulster Irish (the intermediate region). Cunningham applies this same analysis to the Appalachian region as well: the American east coast, Appalachia, and Native Americans. His analysis has the limits of any effort that attempts to connect events and conditions 19 centuries apart and of most efforts to explain Appalachia by focusing on one part of it.

Cunningham's analysis, on the other hand, provides a framework to analyze cultural representations of Appalachia. Figure 2 represents that framework. Between the core and intermediate regions is an economic boundary that the core region penetrates sufficiently to develop economic relations. Between the intermediate and outside regions lies a more rigid political and cultural boundary, like Hadrian's wall demarcating Roman boundaries on the British Isles. The first boundary is permeable. Culture flows from the core region to the intermediate region primarily, and economic goods flow from the intermediate region to the core region primarily. The second boundary is far less permeable and represents the border where, the core group believes, commercial and cultural exchanges are not useful and perhaps dangerous. People venture from the intermediate region and the core region to the outside region primarily to verify the savage nature of the region, the need for rigid boundaries, and the superiority of the other two regions. Virtue is bestowed on those in the outside region who pass the boundaries into one of the other two regions.

Cunningham's borders and regions apply to much of what we already have discussed about

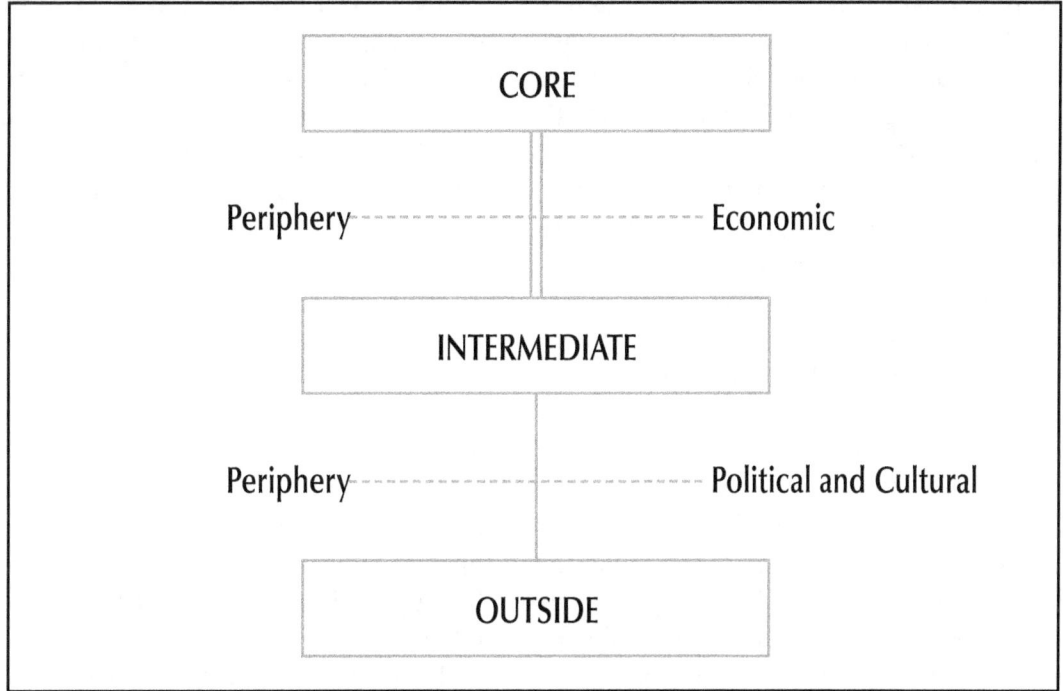

Figure 2 Portrayal of Cunningham's Regions and Boundaries

Appalachian cultural representation. If we keep in mind the economic borders as well as the political and cultural borders disputed by the core and outside regions, we can understand the feud between the Hatfields and the McCoys as a conflict over the permeability of the economic border and the reinforcement of the rigid cultural and political border. Waller's (1988) interpretation of the feud certainly supports this. Cunningham also helps us understand the work of Caudill and Weller. On the one hand, they provide a permeable boundary for the expression of concern of the core region for the intermediate region. On the other hand, Caudill and Weller provide an intermediate region by portraying an outside region where "savages"—insufficiently civilized human beings—have been replaced with "dolts"—insufficiently intelligent or motivated human beings.

Similarly, Cunningham helps explain the shame so many Appalachian professionals feel when they come into contact with the metropolitan core. They are mistaken for "savages" from the outside region. They work hard to pass through the cultural border to the intermediate region as well as through the border to the core. Cunningham ascribes an impaired identity to such people, of which he is one: "a peripheralized people . . . victims of (among other things) distorted rites of passage which reinforce these insecure ego-boundaries and ego-foundations" (Cunningham 1987, p. xxiii).

However useful, Cunningham's analysis has its limits as well. The boundaries, for example, are defined from the core region out. Although this is accurate in terms of power relations, an essential part of culture, it assumes the cultural superiority established by those power relations. Similarly, those boundaries and the individual and collective identities that culture imparts are not static. Even Hadrian's wall was tested, breached, and reinforced.

Like some members of any group, some Appalachians protest their pejorative portrayal: the boundaries of culture that others establish. They may do so vociferously as the coal operator did in the film Rich Land, Poor People. He complained on camera to the camera crew about media portrayals that focused on poverty exclusively. Other Appalachians may protest modestly as one Appalshop character explains in Strangers and Kin, a film about negative stereotypes in Appalachia. He recalled being called to the school auditorium to select a pair of shoes from the hundreds of pairs sent in reaction to a televised documentary on poverty in eastern Kentucky. His father's face expressed disappointment in himself, as provider, and in his son, for accepting someone else's assessment of his need. He never wore those shoes. More recently, local Appalachian residents have used cultural protest in their efforts to block waste dumps or water projects in their communities. They interpreted these projects' premises as assumptions that the people and communities to be affected by the dumps and projects were worth little and better off moved to another location (Cable 1993; Foster 1993).

In addition to challenging the cultural borders established by others, Appalachians also use them and thus reinforce them. Town residents may deny the truth of stereotypes when applied to them, but they may assert their validity when applied to residents outside of town. Likewise, the professional class of the region may accept and extend pejorative portrayals of working-class and low-income residents, as a portion of Caudill's work did. Thus, Cunningham's distinction of a core and outside culture has a counterpart within the intermediate cultural region among people who assert their identity with core values by distinguishing themselves from those whom core values brand "hillbilly" with debilitating human characteristics. Thus, interregional cultural differences have a counterpart in intraregional cultural differences. As Campbell (1993, p. 1) has concluded, "Some Appalachians . . . exhibit modernity by accepting the prevailing stereotypes as valid but only for a certain segment of the population—a segment to which they do not belong."

Despite the negative characteristics embedded in Appalachian stereotypes, some

Appalachians embrace them occasionally. For example, the Appalshop film "Strangers and Kin" shows us "Hillbilly Days" in Pikeville, Kentucky, in which men and women dress up as the media caricatures them and their forebears. Similarly, Hazard, Kentucky, welcomed with open arms, or at least with a downtown parade, the characters of the prime-time television show "The Dukes of Hazzard." If anything could dispel the premise of simple generalizations of Appalachian cultural representations, it would certainly be this event. A coal town of eastern Kentucky, which came within one "z" of the fictional county, feted the cast of a television series filmed in California, set in northern Alabama, but without any African Americans. Hazard, Kentucky, proudly identified with the bungling corruption and tantrums of the political officials and with the bumpkin common sense and decency of the protagonists of the series. Such events portray the human capacity to deflect the shame embedded in stereotypes. Members of a stereotyped group often take the humor aimed at them and laugh at or with those who make the jokes.

More important, such events invite the question, which Batteau (1990) recently examined: "Whose Appalachia is this?" Obviously, as Cunningham and Whisnant make clear, Appalachian cultural representation is a field in which two different cultures conflict. Batteau, Cunningham, and Whisnant make clear that those within the intermediate region learn how to market their culture and that of the outside region. The economic boundary of the core and intermediate regions is permeable to the flow of cultural exchange in both directions when related to economics. Local officials of Columbiana County, Ohio, demonstrated that recently. Originally, they declined to be included among Appalachian counties but reversed themselves in 1991. The switch from concern with stigma to an assertion of "hillbilly" identity came in part with the lost opportunity for federal funds available through participating in programs of the Appalachian Regional Commission. At least one person embraced kinship with West Virginia, a "hillbilly" personality, as well as a "river rat" identity upon the county's entrance into the Appalachian region (Tribe 1993, p. 26).

In answer to his own question, Batteau asserts that Appalachia is a social invention like the cowboy or the Indian. It is one part positive virtues such as self-sufficiency, pioneering spirit, patriotism, independence, and the dignity of making one's humble way despite adversity. It is one part negative images of dependency, failure, retarded economic and human development, and the dismay of humble people having lost their way because of adversity. Appalachian cultural representation is also one part new and one part old. The old part is virulent racism of the 1890s. Appalachia seemed a pool of Anglo-Saxon genes to develop and thus to prove this group's superiority to African Americans and immigrants. The new part is whatever representation seems appropriate to market in a proposal for funding from federal or foundation sources. The region is also both profane and sacred—profane for the human need and environmental destruction in the region and sacred because people and land have been sacrificed for the greed of some and for the well-being of the nation.

In this regard, Galbraith, in his pathbreaking book, The Affluent Society (1958), and in his later reflection on American life, The Culture of Contentment (1992), uses Appalachia as a test of America. His latter book offers a cultural interpretation of America to explain the poverty of the Appalachian region. America's "culture of contentment" entails a majority who are fortunate and favored or who hope to be so, who act on behalf of their own immediate short-term benefit, and who willingly tolerate the need for increased and improved social welfare policies, apparent in places like Appalachia, without doing anything to meet those needs or to achieve those policies (Galbraith 1992). Galbraith illustrates Batteau's conclusion about Appalachian cultural representations: "'Appalachia' is a frame of reference, not a fact." It is a willful association "with a broad array of other texts" (Batteau 1990, p. 200).

CONCLUSION

The practical implications of the cultural representation of Appalachia are made evident throughout this book. They can entail cultural conflict—for example, efforts to change unhealthy behaviors. In addition, the effect of cultural stereotypes on residents of the same Appalachian community will affect their capacity to work together and the membership of coalition efforts. After people learn the painful experience of culture's role in exploitation, they have the opportunity to learn from it and to do better. Two primary strategies deal with negative cultural stereotypes: to protest those that others use and to do better ourselves (Speer 1993).

Behind these practical difficulties are the profoundly complex factors that create, maintain, and adapt a wide assortment of Appalachian cultural representations. Obviously, any community-based, problem-solving intervention needs to start with the history and culture of the community in which it is occurring. In Appalachia, as in every other region, this means inquiring about and uncovering those specifics. Communities in Appalachian New York vary widely from those in Appalachian Mississippi. Similarly, adjoining counties may vary as well and require different approaches in community-based problem solving because of different histories and cultural adaptations.

CHAPTER 2

The Sociology of Southern Appalachia

by David S. Walls and Dwight B. Billings

Sociologists have been fascinated by the Appalachians ever since George Vincent of the University of Chicago took a four-day horseback ride through Breathitt, Perry, and Knott Counties in eastern Kentucky in 1898. Urging study of "this curious social survival . . . now being modified so rapidly," Vincent concluded his descriptive and impressionistic account, "Let students of sociology leave their books and at first hand in the Cumberlands deal with the phenomena of a social order arrested at a relatively early state of evolution."[1] Setting aside questions about the accuracy of Vincent's characterization of the region as a retarded frontier, we can see in his article two themes which predominate in sociological studies of Appalachia from his day to ours: social change and social problems.

Vincent acknowledged his debt to such writers of the "local color movement" as Mary Murfree and John Fox, Jr., for being the first to recognize the Southern Mountains as a distinctive subcultural region. The "discovery" of the Southern Appalachians is itself a problem in the sociology of knowledge and has been addressed by historian Henry Shapiro in *Appalachia on Our Minds*,[2] a brilliant interpretation of the emergence of a national consciousness of Southern Appalachia in the period from 1875 to 1920. Herbert Blumer's comment could well apply to Vincent (and many others) in regard to Appalachia: "Sociological recognition follows in the wake of societal recognition, veering with the winds of the public identification of social problems."[3]

THEORIES OF SOCIAL CHANGE AND SOCIAL PROBLEMS

The themes of social change, social problems, and the response of private and public social policy underlie the major social surveys of the Southern Appalachian region: John C. Campbell's *Southern Highlander and His Homeland* in 1921, the U.S. Department of Agriculture's *Economic and Social Problems and Conditions of the Southern Appalachians* in 1935, the section on the "Southern Appalachian Coal Plateaus" in the Study of Population Redistribution in 1936, the Ford Foundation supported study *The Southern Appalachian Region: A Survey* in 1962, and the various studies and annual reports of the

---

Source: Reprinted from *Appalachian Journal*, vol. 5, no. 1 (Autumn 1977, pp. 131–144). Copyright © Appalachian State University/Appalachian Journal. Used by permission.

Appalachian Regional Commission since 1965.[4] These studies illustrate a major accomplishment of the sociology of Appalachia: the analysis of demographic data from census statistics, including population changes, fertility rates, incomes, unemployment, housing, health, and so on.

Surprisingly, little systematic attention has been devoted by sociologists of Appalachia to fundamental theories of social change or models that explain regional poverty and underdevelopment. Tacit assumptions about the process of social change are more common than explicit models of the roots of regional problems and strategies to overcome the area's difficulties. Description, explanation, and prescription are intertwined in many studies and are not often clearly distinguished. Yet over the years a variety of arguments have been advanced to account for what is variously described as the backwardness, poverty, underdevelopment, and resistance to change of the Appalachian region and its people.

Genes vs. Environment. In the late nineteenth century, historian John Fiske implied a genetic basis for Appalachian poverty and backwardness by suggesting the poor class of mountaineers were the descendants of convicts and indentured servants. The argument of genetic deficiency was elaborated in the 1920s by Arthur Estabrook and Nathaniel Hirsch and revived recently by Harry Caudill.[5] In contrast, the geographic circumstances of isolation and poor communication were emphasized at the turn of the century by William Frost and Ellen Semple.[6] One objective of John Campbell in The Southern Highlander was to refute Fiske's argument by providing a correct record of the origins and current status of mountain people and by emphasizing an environmental explanation of mountain problems.[7] In recent years genetic and geographical explanations have generally been superseded by sociocultural and economic theories. During the 1960s, three models were drawn upon to explain Appalachian poverty and underdevelopment: the subculture of poverty, regional development, and internal colonialism models. Each of these three current models was first discovered in the context of underdevelopment in the Third World and applied by analogy to the Appalachian case.

Subculture of Poverty. The subculture of poverty model identifies the internal deficiencies of the lower-class subculture as the source of the problem. Oscar Lewis is the social scientist most closely identified with this model, and the most widely read exposition of the model applied to Appalachia is Jack Weller's Yesterday's People, which borrows an analytic framework from Herbert Gans.[8] The subculture of poverty model suggests remedial programs of education, social casework, and clinical psychology. Other studies of Appalachian culture in these terms include David Louff's *Appalachia's Children,* Norman Polansky's *Roots of Futility,* and various articles by Richard Ball.[9]

This model in general has been subjected to devastating criticism, and Steve Fisher has criticized Weller's application of this model to Appalachia.[10] In an empirical test, sociologist Dwight Billings has shown the model to be of little value in explaining the lack of economic development in the mountain section of North Carolina and the contrasting industrialization of the piedmont. Ironically, it was just when the distinctiveness of the Southern Appalachian traditional subculture was fading that the subculture of poverty model was popularized and applied to the region.[11]

The pejorative viewpoint on Appalachian culture has been answered by an affirmative approach in works from John and Olive Campbell through Loyal Jones' essay on Appalachian values. Mike Maloney and Ben Huelman have contrasted the affirmative and pejorative approaches in their essay, "Humanism, Scientism, and the Southern Mountaineer."[12] With the humanistic tradition, in their terms, are Robert Coles, John Fetterman, Tony Dunbar, Kathy Kahn, and John Stephenson, who use their subjects' own words to characterize Appalachian life-worlds.[13] Their descriptions of individuals and families manage to capture the strengths as well as the shortcomings of mountaineers and the diversity of personality types within some common subcultural themes.

The subculture of poverty model can be seen as only one approach within a broader framework of explanations rooted in the tradition of cultural idealism. Affirmative cultural approaches toward Southern Appalachia, as exemplified by Frost and the Campbells, are the obverse side of the coin from the pejorative tradition of the subculture of poverty school. The regionalism of the 1930s, as personified by Howard Odum and others, followed in the tradition of affirmative cultural idealism and looked to ties to the land and a sense of place, combined with planning, for regional revitalization. As John Friedmann points out, the new regionalism of the 1960s discarded the grounding in cultural idealism in favor of a regional development model resting within the contemporary technocratic image and ideology of science.[14]

Regional Development. Although the literature on development includes disciplines from social psychology to social ecology, the most influential stream derives from neo-classical economics as amended by central place theory.[15] The resulting regional development model is concerned with providing economic and social overhead capital, training people for skills for new industrial and service jobs, facilitating migration, and promoting the establishment or relocation of privately-owned industries through a growth center. Niles Hansen is probably the best known academic proponent of this approach. The major attempt to apply the model within the United States is the work of the Appalachian Regional Commission (ARC) and its associated programs.[16]

A major sociological contribution to the regional development model is the notion of a modernizing elite as the agent of the developmental process. H. Dudley Plunkett and Mary Jean Bowman elaborate this idea in *Elites and Change in the Kentucky Mountains*. They identify the "interstitial person" as the "cultural bridge" between traditional and modernizing groups and investigate such key occupational groups as bankers, lawyers, public officials, clergy, physicians, and schoolteachers to determine their relative commitments to change. In general, Plunkett and Bowman found the "ministering professionals"—clergy, physicians, and teachers—to have the most modern outlook: businessmen to be intermediate; and the local administrative elite, the "gerontocracy" of bankers, lawyers, and politicians to be the most traditional.[17] The ARC strategy appears to follow the Plunkett and Bowman suggestion of cooperating with the modernizing professionals to coopt or outmaneuver the traditional business elites and the old county political machines. The basic structure for this strategy on the local level is the multi-county Local Development District, which serves as a mechanism for arriving at consensus among regional elites. Through the dual federal-state structure of the ARC, the interests of regional and national elites are reconciled.

With its emphasis on mainstream economic theory and the technical aspects of development, the regional development model lays claim to being a scientific, value-free, non-controversial approach. As such, it is an effective means of providing additional resources to the region without affecting the existing structure of resource control. Actions taken by regional and national planners are defended as technical decisions, rather than political choices among alternative courses of development. Political sociology calls attention to the possibility that the most important decisions may be the "non-decision": the questions that are never raised and the subjects that never make the public agenda. Examples include public ownership of the region's natural resources and worker or community owned and controlled industry.[18]

Internal Colonialism. The issues of power and privilege in Appalachia are seldom faced squarely by the subculture of poverty and regional development advocates. In reaction to this obvious shortcoming, academics and activists looked for a model that emphasized inequality and exploitation. They hit upon the internal colonialism model for reasons that had much to do with the focus of the New Left in the 1960s—imperialism abroad and oppression of racial minorities at home. As applied to Appalachia, the internal colonialism model has been used to examine the process by which dominant outside industrial interests established control and continue to prevent autonomous development of the subordinate internal colony. The model suggests the need for an anticolonial movement and a radical restructuring of society, with the redistribution of resources to the poor and powerless.

In his best selling 1962 study *Night Comes to the Cumberlands,* Harry Caudill makes only a passing reference to colonialism; by 1965 he begins to use the internal colonial designation. The theme was quickly picked up by activists and radical intellectuals in the Central Appalachian area, particularly the group associated with the Peoples' Appalachian Research Collective and its journal, *Peoples' Appalachia.*[19]

Helen Lewis and her associates have attempted a detailed application to Appalachia of Robert Blauner's model of the process of internal colonization of black Americans. In this analysis, such institutions as the Appalachian family and church emerge as not simply survivals of an earlier traditional subculture but also as defensive institutions whose "closed" characteristics are in part formed in resistance to the process of colonization. By emphasizing such values as "equality, non-competitiveness, and family-neighborhood solidarity," the family and the church resist the social change that would integrate the region into the American mainstream.[20]

Much of the attraction of the internal colonialism model, including its application to Appalachia, derives from its powerful analysis of the destruction of indigenous culture in the process of establishing and maintaining domination over the colonized group. It has also performed a valuable service by focusing attention on the acquisition of the raw materials of the region by outside corporate interests and on the exploitation of the local work force and community at large resulting from the removal of the region's natural resources for the benefit of absentee owners.

Although the internal colonialism model has raised important questions about wealth, power, and exploitation in central Appalachia, it may not offer the most satisfactory characterization of the situation of the region. The analogy with racial minorities in America has serious limitations in any strict definition of internal colonialism.[21] The involuntary entry into the United States of enslaved blacks from Africa or the conquered Native American tribes and the Mexican people of the Southwest presents a substantially different situation from that of most Appalachians. Barriers to the assimilation of Appalachians into mainstream society—prejudice against "hillbillies"—are based on bias against the lower classes, not against all the people of the region. The historical development of Appalachia since the expansion of industrial capitalism may present a better example of class domination than Colonial domination.[22]

Toward a More Comprehensive Theory of Social Change in Appalachia. A comprehensive theory of social change in Appalachia must synthesize and integrate a humanistic approach to culture, the technical aspects of regional development, and an appropriate critique of domination at the present period. Some outlines of such a theory emerge from the work of Frankfurt School theorist Jürgen Habermas. For Habermas there are three fundamental conditions or media through which social systems are maintained: interaction, work, and power or domination. All human societies use these means to resolve the problems of preserving life and culture. Corresponding to each of these media are the human "interests" in mutual understanding, technical control, and "emancipation from seemingly 'natural' constraint."[23] A solution to the problems of Appalachian poverty and underdevelopment would have to be concerned with each of the three modes of culture, technique, and domination. Habermas' distinction provides a basis for viewing cultural adaptation, technical development, and redistribution of power as potentially complementary aspects of social development.

We suggest the history of the Appalachian region is best understood in the context of industrial capitalist development. Currently, Appalachia must be analyzed in the context of advanced capitalism in the United States. In some instances (analyzing the role of the Japanese steel industry in providing capital for opening new coal mines in the region, for example), we may have to expand our horizon to the framework of the world capitalist system. In a recent work Habermas analyzes advanced capitalist societies in terms of their economic, administrative (state), and legitimation systems and the resulting class structures. This framework prompts us to examine the competitive and monopolistic sectors of private industry, the role of state expenditures, the legitimation of the system and the containment of rebellion, and the full complexity of the class structure of the region.[24] It may be fruitful to view Southern Appalachia as a peripheral region, rather than an internal colony, within an advanced capitalist society.[25]

"MIDDLE-RANGE" ISSUES IN THE SOCIOLOGY OF SOUTHERN APPALACHIA

At a less comprehensive level of social theory, in the "middle-range" of sociological investigation, base-line studies have been made in several areas. We have substantial knowledge of kinship and community structures, cultural configurations, and demographic changes. We have much less complete knowledge of Appalachian patterns of social stratification and politics. It is useful to summarize these studies and to point out deficiencies in our knowledge.

Class, Status, and Power in Appalachia. As noted above, the subculture model and the regional development model of Appalachian change have both diverted attention away from certain aspects of social structure and politics and redirected attention to issues of cultural and psychological "modernity"—this, despite the fact that Appalachia was born modern. Two misconceptions about the traditional subculture deserve comment. The traditional subculture of the Southern Appalachians should not be characterized as either a poverty subculture or as a peasant culture. The pre-industrial, pioneer way of life cannot be equated with a subculture of poverty as described by Oscar Lewis; there is no evidence that traditional mountain families felt helpless, dependent, or inferior.[26] The analogy to a peasantry has been used in two senses, both in reference to the traditional subculture and to the type of domination during the company town era.[27] Neither analogy is accurate. Nineteenth-century mountaineers were not descendants of a peasant people, but the children and grandchildren of eighteenth century colonists, most of whom had been landless wage-earners from an agricultural and mercantile capitalist country about to enter into the industrial revolution. In sharp contrast to the *Gemeinschaft* solidarity of traditional peasant society, the Appalachian mountaineer was already the quintessential modern individualist. Further, the situation of the miner in the company town is typical of social relations in the early stage of oligopoly capitalism and should be designated as such, not as a condition of peasantry.

Inappropriate cultural models—as they fix attention on "rich Appalachia" and "poor Appalachia," on "traditional Appalachia" and "modern Appalachia"—obscure the region's complex pattern of social stratification. The expansion of state expenditures has helped create sizeable intermediate groupings of public workers (in education, local government, and public services) and workers in industries heavily subsidized by public funds (health services particularly). These elements of the "new working-class" have taken their places alongside such long-established groups as coal miners, workers in small factories, small farmers, country merchants, county-seat retailers, bankers, professionals, independent coal operators, and managers for the nationally-based coal companies in the monopolistic sector, in addition to the household workers, the welfare poor, and others outside the standard labor force. The occupational structure is obviously complex, and its changes need to be analyzed over time, particularly in relation to changes in the coal industry and the growth of state expenditures.

We have no studies of industrial communities in the mountains and, consequently, we have few accounts of stratification in mining communities and county-seat towns. Rural stratification has frequently been over-looked as well,[28] but some good studies have been made. John Stephenson has pictured a four-level structure in "Shiloh," and Schwarzweller, Brown, and Mangalam[29] have identified a clearly developed stratification system in "Beech Creek," despite the fact that they were studying poor families. Social status differences in Beech Creek were manifested in family reputation, visiting, marital exchanges, and territorial locations. Lower status people retained their ascribed family status—in the authors' words their "inherited stigma"—despite personal achievements. This suggests that social factors which influence interaction in mountain communities across status boundaries have not been sufficiently studied. Such factors have important consequences for power and participation in local communities and thus for social and economic mobility.

One of the authors of this essay (Billings) first encountered the process of stratification when he attended grade school in a Southern West Virginia county-seat town. School property included two buildings and students were segregated by their fathers' occupations. "Coal Camp" students were routinely assigned to an annex, ostensibly because of "special learning difficulties," although every year two or three were assigned to the main building. In the fourth grade, Billings observed that one of these children always turned red and buried her face in her hands when the teacher called on her to participate in class. This same child was once stood up before the class and her chapped hands were shown to her classmates. The teacher explained that her father could not afford to buy her handcream and, in missionary language, she asked if one of the other children would share her bounty and bring her some cream. The undertaker's daughter did. Later, in her absence, the class was told that this was the same child who brought lice into the classroom.

This story suggests that being poor involves a social identity which is learned early and enforced by informal relationships in the local community. We know little about the rule-governed interactions—in the school, the work place, the welfare office, the voting place—which condition the performances of those defined as "the poor" in the mountains. Nor do we know much about the group with whom they have the most direct contact, the mountain middle class, for the latter have been rarely studied. Sociologists who have studied the middle class, such as Plunkett and Bowman, have been chiefly interested in their attitudes. The mountain middle class is typically viewed as a "cultural bridge" between the rural community and mass society. Their role as "gatekeeper," a better functional analogy, has been ignored and their influence on education, social services, political participation, and the economy has not been fully grasped. In fact, community power structure studies in Southern Appalachia are practically non-existent, although we have had Floyd Hunter's work as an exemplar for over 20 years, and a vast amount of subsequent literature.[30]

Richard Ball reported on the power structure of a northern West Virginia mining county; Rod Harless reported on a county in southern West Virginia.[31] Harless found that the county political elite, consisting of bankers and lawyers, were also on retainer for absentee corporations. Harless, however, used only the positional study method, not the reputational or decision-making case study methods. His work is of limited use for understanding the actual exercise of power and influence although it suggests a political structure similar to those found in other economically peripheral or dependent regions.[32] The middle-class role in county politics has also been discussed by Harry Caudill, Richard Couto, Tony Dunbar, and in Huey Perry's "They'll Cut Off Your Project," a description of confrontation in West Virginia during the War on Poverty.[33]

Scholars who developed the colonial model have focused attention on another social group, absentee owners, who are influential in the life of the region, and in the politics of natural resource development. For example, Harless tried to identify a West Virginia ownership establishment and Richard Diehl[34] described an "Appalachian Energy Elite." A field of growing importance is the sociology of natural resource use. The social impact of the Army Corps of Engineers' dam building is beginning to be studied. The social and economic costs of Appalachian coal production have been explored in a series of reports by the Appalachian Resources Project at the University of Tennessee. Si Kahn has opened a discussion of the impact of Forest Service policies on the region.[35] Sue Johnson and Rabel Burdge have outlined a methodology for sociologists making contributions to Environmental Impact Statements under the National Environmental Policy Act of 1969. Another avenue for investigating the social impact of a disaster is explored by Kai Erikson's study of the destruction of community in the wake of the Buffalo Creek Flood.[36]

For the most part, these studies, like the community literature, fail to analyze the actual use of power and influence by absentee owners. An important exception is John Gaventa's analysis of the American Association, an English land-holding corporation in eastern Kentucky and Tennessee.[37] On a related theme, the increasing coordination of government and business in resource development has been described by David Whisnant and by Harry Caudill in the *Watches of the Night*.[38]

Surprisingly little attention has been paid to racial and ethnic minority groups, a shortcoming which has bolstered the old stereotype of Appalachia as a bastion of Anglo-Saxon stock. Racial minorities in Southern Appalachia include blacks, Native Americans, and mixed-race groups. Blacks numbered approximately 1.3 million of the total Appalachian population of 18.2 million according to the 1970 census, some 7.3 percent of the population in the 13-state region as defined by the ARC.[39] The few studies that have been made concerning black Appalachians have been concerned primarily with their participation in the coal industry.[40] Blacks composed a substantial proportion of the work force in coal mining in the Southern states between 1890 and 1930. Since that time the proportion of black miners has declined. The mechanization of the industry that began in the 1950s hit particularly hard at the black miner, who did not receive an equal share of the jobs operating continuous miners and other heavy equipment. As employment in the coal industry declined, blacks were laid off in disproportionate numbers. The increase in strip mining also worked against blacks, who rarely obtained jobs with stripping firms. Black Appalachians have been migrating out of the region at a greater rate than whites.

The Eastern Band of Cherokee Indians is the only organized group of Native Americans living in the Southern Appalachian region. Until recently, the only thorough study of the Eastern Cherokees had been conducted in the late 1950s by the Cross-Cultural Laboratory at the University of North Carolina. The Special Cherokee Issue of the *Appalachian Journal* in 1975, edited by Burt Purrington, has added considerable new material on the Eastern Cherokees.[41] The four counties in western North Carolina which include the Eastern Cherokee reservation lands had a total Indian population of 3,937 in the 1970 census. Several hundred additional Indians live in the North Carolina Piedmont and eastern Tennessee.

Ten major mixed-race or triracial (white, black, and Native American ancestry) groups have been identified in the eastern United States. Two of these, the "Melungeons" and the

"Guineas," reside within the Southern Appalachian region. The Melungeons of Tennessee continue to give rise to a considerable quantity of mythology, despite the sober scholarship of Edward Price in the early 1950s. There is little up-to-date information on either group, although a study is underway on the Guineas of West Virginia.[42] An attempt was made to count the mixed-race peoples in the 1950 census, but the figures are highly suspect.[43] Research is needed to determine to what extent these groups have been maintained or have been assimilated.

As with blacks, studies of European ethnic groups in Southern Appalachia have been conducted mainly in terms of their association with the coal industry.[44] And with the notable exception of Kathy Kahn's *Hillbilly Women,* little systematic attention has been given to mountain women.

Finally, in the last few years some excellent theoretical work on social movement organization has been done by sociologists, and we have two exemplary case studies of CORE and SDA.[45] But for Appalachian social movements, social scientists have not kept up with the journalists in describing how occupants of class and status positions organize for cooperative and political action. Brit Hume's *Death and the Mines* provides information on the Black Lung Association and the Miners for Democracy movements. The War on Poverty in Appalachia has prompted many books.[46] David Whisnant has provided historical interpretations of the Council of the Southern Mountains and the Congress for Appalachian Development, and Frank Adams has written a history of the Highlander Center.[47] Most of the literature on the Tennessee Valley Authority written since Philip Selznick's classic *TVA and the Grass Roots* has been historical rather than analytical.[48] Little evaluative research has been done on either the War on Poverty programs or the Appalachian Regional Commission. Attempts by community organizers to create an Appalachian identity among unemployed out migrants in urban contexts and to adapt their communities to the model of inner-city ethnic group politics also deserve more attention.[49]

Culture and Community in Appalachia. Since the time of Frost and the Campbells, students of the Southern Appalachians have been attempting to characterize the subculture of the region. In the major effort to survey the extent to which the traditional subculture has persisted, Thomas Ford in 1962 defined four themes: individualism and self-reliance, traditionalism, fatalism, and fundamentalism. Of these, the people questioned showed a significant difference from national norms only in the direction of greater fundamentalism.[50] It is not clear whether subcultural differences that still persist are distinctive of Southern Appalachia rather than of the rural South, of the rural United States generally, or, as a cultural geographer has suggested, of the Upland South.[51]

Too often, social scientists have erroneously sought to measure Appalachian culture against some standard of urban, middle-class values. This is especially a problem when the former is pejoratively pitted against the latter which is seen as an indicator of "modernity" and, implicitly, of moral health. This prevents an understanding of Appalachian culture in its own terms. In Eugene Genovese's *Roll, Jordon, Roll,* an analysis of slave culture in the American South, and in Richard Sennett and Jonathan Cobb's *The Hidden Injuries of Class,* an analysis of ethnic, working-class culture in contemporary Boston, we have exemplary treatments of the dialectical relationship between class position and culture in history.[52] Unfortunately we lack such a comprehensive historical study of Appalachian culture and society, although James Brown and Helen Lewis have provided much insight.

Brown summarizes the orientation of the preindustrial Appalachian culture in three themes: familism (social interaction), puritanism (belief system), and individualism (personality system).[53] In *Mountain Families in Transition* the authors abstract cultural traits from their behavioral expressions which exactly counter the pathogenic qualities so often attributed to the culture of "yesterday's people." In a brilliant article entitled "Family, Religion and Colonialism in Central Appalachia; or Bury My Rifle at Big Stone Gap," Helen Lewis, Sue Kobak, and Linda Johnson interpret more recent developments in Appalachian culture as a response to "the process of colonialization as it occurred in the Central Appalachians."[54] Family and church institutions, in particular, "became defensive and reverted inward in order to protect members from the sudden influence which came with the development of industrialization." Their work suggests that seen in this context, as a localized response beginning at the turn of the century to the national mobilization of population and resources in America to achieve maximum capitalist industrial development, contemporary Appalachian culture can no longer be seen as that of an "arrested frontier." Rather, one sees functional parallels between contemporary Appalachian culture and other such reactive movements as populism in the South, the emergence of ethnic communities in the industrial Northeast, the flight of the white middle class to suburbia in the 1950s in order to preserve the values of small town and family living,[55] the emergence of a "counterculture" among their children in the 1960s, the subsequent flight of many of these children underground or to Canada to avoid the Vietnam War, the recent protest among working-class communities against busing, and even the opposition to imposed textbooks in the rural sections of West Virginia's Kanawha Valley industrial region. All these may be seen as responses to centralizing tendencies of mobilization and massification.

Studies of communities in Southern Appalachia are less advanced than is first apparent. We have some excellent studies of isolated agricultural communities: Marion Pearsall's *Little Smokey Ridge,* Brown's "Beech Creek." But we also have studies of very poor communities presented as typical: Rena Gazaway's "Duddie's Branch," and Bill Surface's *The Hollow.*[56] And then we have three studies of Celo, North Carolina, done in the early and mid-1960s which make little or no reference to each other.[57]

Studies by John Stephenson, Helen Lewis, and others demonstrate the variety of occupational groupings and life-styles within rural communities.[58] Art Gallaher has suggested a typology of communities ranging from extremely isolated rural, less isolated rural with some stores and services, company towns, county seat towns, and major urban areas.[59] The diversity of family, life style, and community types is apparent, in contrast to the stereotypes of the uniform subculture of poverty on the one hand, and the polarization of Appalachian society into the rich and the poor on the other.[60] Among aspects of Appalachian culture and community, family organization has received much attention. The importance of the extended family and kinship groups has been noted in most studies of rural regions in Appalachia, in comparison with the relative isolation of the nuclear family in mainstream society. Brown's study of "Beech Creek" over a thirty-year period has made the greatest contribution to the study of mountain families during the great migration out of the region between 1940 and 1970.

The presentation and analysis of census data on the Appalachian region has long been used to describe the characteristics of the population, the differences within the region, and its lag behind the rest of the nation. Campbell presents data from the 1910 census in *The Southern Highlander;* the USDA study presents data through the early 1930s; the Ford study analyzes the data from 1940 to 1960, and Brown has analyzed the 1970 census.[61] Gordon DeJong has made the most detailed analysis of fertility decline in the region.[62] The Annual Reports of the ARC bring the income and employment figures up to date. Recently efforts have been made to assess changes in the "quality of life" in the region.[63]

The study of migration out of and into the Appalachians has been developed in considerable detail. Migration from the region has been a feature since the early 1800s; overlooking this pattern contributes to an exaggerated sense of the isolation of the region during the mid-1800s. People left the mountain areas of Kentucky, Tennessee, and the Carolinas and made their way to the Ozarks, southern Illinois, and Oklahoma.[64] A longstanding migration stream from two sources in the Southern Appalachians to two areas of settlement in western Washington state, two thousand miles away, has been described in detail in Woodrow Clevinger.[65] The migration began around 1880, in connection with the timber industry, hit a peak between 1900 and 1917, and continues to a limited extent even to this day. During the 1930s the central Appalachians experienced a net in-migration stream.[66] The work of Clevinger, Brown, and others has demonstrated the importance of the family system in the migration process. While the major migration streams from the region are known, much remains to be done to identify the streams on a detailed, local, or county level. Related to the literature on Appalachian migration is a variety of material on occupational adjustment to industrial work.[67]

An obvious deficiency in the sociological literature on the Appalachian community is the analysis of work. Despite the growing literature on the "single industry community," we have no good studies on industrial communities in the mountains. The only study of a coal mining community in the United States is Herman Lantz's "Coal Town" in southern Illinois.[68] With the exception of the work of Lewis and Knipe, and studies by Ronald Althouse and Keith Dix, little has been done on the industrial sociology of the coal industry by social scientists. Investigative journalists have accomplished far more in analyzing developments in the coal industry, mine disaster, and the everyday life of coal miners.[69] A fascinating problem in this area of industrial sociology is explaining the success of unionization in the coalfields and its failure in the textile mills. No comparative studies of coal and textile communities have been made, despite the assertion that both share similar subculture and situation of domination.[70]

Toward a Sociology of the Appalachian Future. Much of the research on Southern Appalachia has sought either to discover a romantic past or to proclaim "the eve of an astonishing development."[71] Instead, we need hard sociological thinking about an Appalachian future. For this we need a more adequate historical society in order to recover an authentic mountain past and to gain a critical perspective on current developments. We also need a more comprehensive sociology of culture in order to articulate the values and goals of Appalachian people, especially those who otherwise lack an institutional basis from which to be heard. Such people have not often been listened to by missionaries, developers, and bureaucrats. Finally, we urgently need a study of the landowning and energy-getting elites in Appalachia whose plans, about which we are always so ignorant, often seem inexorable. The likely emergence of a national energy policy and the importance of coal in that policy make this research agenda and the timely voice of Appalachian people all the more imperative.

CHAPTER 13

Beyond Isolation and Homogeneity: Diversity and the History of Appalachia

by Ronald L. Lewis

Appalachia is a region without a formal history. Born in the fertile minds of late-nineteenth-century local color writers, "Appalachia" was invented in the caricatures and atmospheric landscapes of the escapist fiction they penned to entertain the emergent urban middle class. The accuracy of these stories and travelogues, the dominant idioms of this genre, generated little or no critical evaluation of their characterizations of either mountain people or the landscape itself.

If local color writing in the Appalachian motif must have a beginning, it would be with Will Wallace Harney's 1873 travelogue, "A Strange Land and Peculiar People," published in *Lippincott's Magazine*.[1] His emphasis on physical and cultural isolation was greatly magnified over the next two decades by subsequent writers. The publication in 1899 of Berea College president William Goodell Frost's famous article, "Our Contemporary Ancestors in the Southern Mountains," signified the maturity of the concept of Appalachia as a spatially and culturally remote remnant of a bygone day. From this essay, only one of Frost's storehouse of appeals for support to finance his missionary work in the mountains, came some of the most widely recognized phrases applied to Appalachian mountain dwellers. They were "our contemporary ancestors," our "eighteenth century neighbors" who had just awakened from a long "Rip Van Winkle sleep," pure Anglo-Saxons "beleaguered by nature" in "Appalachian America," one of "God's grand divisions."[2] Frost the publicist certainly knew how to turn a phrase.

"Local color" Appalachia reached its apogee in the novels of John Fox, Jr., undoubtedly the most popular author of the genre. Scholars recognize that Fox was a major figure in the creation of Appalachian "otherness," but Darlene Wilson has shown most emphatically how self-serving were Fox's creations. Declaring his writing "deliberate acts of self-creation and self-mythologizing," Wilson's research in family papers reveals the direct linkage between Fox's fictional images and his "role as a publicist for absentee mineral developers" who, along with their agent, Fox's older half-brother James, were involved in the development of the coal industry in central Appalachia. John Fox Jr. perpetrated and then perpetuated the myth of Appalachian otherness to facilitate absentee corporate hegemony by

Source: From *Confronting Appalachian Stereotypes: Back Talk from an American Region* by Billings, Norman & Ledford, eds. Copyright © 1999 by University Press of Kentucky. Reprinted by permission.

marginalizing indigenous residents economically and politically. In short, for Fox (and how many others?) "Appalachia" was a willful creation and not merely the product of literary imagination.[3]

This fictional representation became accepted and then reified as "history" by subsequent reporters, scholars, and policy makers into what Henry Shapiro has called the "myth of Appalachia." As Shapiro and Allen Batteau show in their work on the "invention" of Appalachia, the idea of Appalachia as a homogeneous region physically, culturally, and economically isolated from mainstream America has its genesis in fiction. In fact, "much of what is believed to be known about the life and people" of Appalachia actually is "knowledge about a complex intertextual reality" that treats the "diverse preindustrial localities in the southern mountains as if each were representative of a single, regionwide folk society."[4] This view has persisted in part because so little formal written history about preindustrial Appalachia exists to provide a measure of empirical authenticity. However, if we examine the region's economic evolution from the perspective of rural nineteenth-century America, without assuming prior knowledge of its fictional existence, or the industrial developments that were to come, it is clear that much of Appalachia was neither unusually isolated, physically or culturally, nor was its population uniformly more homogeneous than that of other sections of rural America.[5]

Acknowledging the risk of exaggeration, much recent scholarship either refutes or greatly revises the standard perspective of preindustrial Appalachia as an isolated frontier. This is particularly true if isolation is understood as the absence of commercial or cultural linkages with regional and/or national markets. Appalachians were not "precapitalist" either, strictly speaking, for even the earliest settlers emigrated from areas where capitalist terms of exchange were well understood. No one generalization holds true for the entire region or over time.

Historically, writers have assumed that the conditions they found in the twentieth century were held over from earlier frontier days. In fact, geographer Gene Wilhelm rejects the notion that early Appalachia was a land without commercial or cultural communications with the world beyond the hollow. According to Wilhelm, "the Appalachian region has been an admixture of cultural contact and socioeconomic enterprise rather than a bastion of isolated individuals and a slow sequence of economic development" as numerous new writers have generally insisted. Wilhelm has argued that "the idea that the Appalachian Mountains acted as a physical barrier, either for the people living within the mountain region, or for those individuals trying to cross them, hardly stands up against the evidence at hand."[6] For example, the Blue Ridge Mountains between Front Royal and Waynesboro, Virginia, were marked out by a complex series of trails and trade routes, traversed by Indians for hundreds of years, even before the Europeans came. Before roads were built, horse and wagon trails crossed the mountains north and south, east and west. During the nineteenth century, innumerable public roads and private pikes connected the region internally and externally. Wilhelm correctly points out that animal drovers provide an excellent example of mountaineers who traveled the lines of trade and cultural transmission connecting the mountains with local and urban markets. Cattle dealers journeyed out to the markets and brought back goods, cash, and ideas. Lowland culture bearers, such as lawyers, doctors, seasonal teachers, tax collectors, circuit preachers, peddlers, salesmen, and mailmen, traveled the same avenues of transportation and trade into the mountains. One of the first backward linkages settlers fought for were postal roads to connect them with the lowland population centers. The high level of newspaper and periodical subscriptions, and later catalog circulation, in the mountains suggests an ongoing desire for knowledge of and goods from the broader world. Wilhelm insists that "geographical isolation for the mountain folk is a myth."[7]

Several major works which subsequently dealt with the topic presented variations on Wilhelm's theme. Ronald D Eller agreed with Wilhelm in general but concluded that travel was nonetheless always difficult and ensured a relative isolation.[8] Steven Hahn's study of up-country Georgia between 1850 and 1890 argues that during the antebellum era local farmers were isolated from the external markets and so they relied on community networks, but after the railroad penetrated the region they became increasingly dependent on the cotton export market.[9] Lacy Ford came to a different conclusion in his study of antebellum up-country South Carolina. While yeomen farmers produced a subsistence first, they also participated in the market economy after the arrival of the railroad in 1850.[10] Although Durwood Dunn generally infers that Cades Cove, which is located in the Tennessee Smokies, was isolated and self-reliant during the early years, he emphasizes that "this isolation was always relative" and shows that during the antebellum years Cove people had relatively ready access to regional markets.[11] Most recently, Wilma Dunaway argued that Appalachia was a peripheral region of an emergent world capitalist system and was linked to that system of exchange as a supplier of raw materials from its inception.[12]

Conversely, Altina Waller's Tug Fork, the borderland between Kentucky and West Virginia where the Hatfield-McCoy feud occurred, was isolated in every respect before the area was opened up in 1889 by the railroad. There were no towns, and county seats were physically isolated from even regional markets. Unlike the Blue Ridge, up-country Georgia, or Cades Cove, Tennessee, there was little migration into this section after 1840, and trade beyond the mountains was "almost non-existent."[13] Moreover, Dwight Billings, Kathleen Blee, and Louis Swanson found that Beech Creek residents of eastern Kentucky remained an isolated people "still living a relatively pre-capitalist life on the eve of World War II." In Beech Creek, "isolation permitted an independent economy to persist in the Appalachian mountains long after it had vanished elsewhere in the United States." Even here, however, national market forces made it increasingly difficult to sustain the local economy.[14]

David Hsiung's study of northeastern Tennessee called for a more critical examination of "isolation" as a conceptual construct and suggested that focusing on the early period between 1780 and 1835 may provide a broader context for measuring Appalachian isolation relative to the rest of backcountry America in the nineteenth century. Not surprisingly, he concluded that isolation was a relative concept both temporally and spatially. In the Revolutionary era residents used the elaborate trail system that fed into the Great Warrior Path and Boone's Trail in northeastern Tennessee. The crude roads made travel and trade difficult and also sparked the creation of new counties so that residents could be closer to the county seat. Residents in these counties were not cut off from the state capital, but clearly they believed themselves to be isolated by poor access to government and the markets. Hsiung noted that it was the "psychic power of physical separation" that motivated county building among the people. By 1820, however, the roads connecting county seats were carrying wagonloads of goods from Philadelphia and other eastern cities into these counties in a brisk interregional trade.[15]

Tracy McKenzie qualifies the development trajectory implied in Hsiung's characterization of northeastern Tennessee. Using 1860 census data, McKenzie has compared the economies of the three grand divisions of western, middle, and eastern Tennessee and found great economic variation among them. Only the mountain counties did not rely on slavery for agricultural production. Even within the three sample Appalachian Tennessee counties (Johnson, Greene, and Grainger) McKenzie found significant differences in their linkages to the regional market. Johnson County farmers "were probably as close to total isolation from the surrounding region as it was possible to be in the nineteenth century," for there were few roads and the railroad did not penetrate the area until the mid-1890s. Grainger and Greene Counties are located in the Valley of East Tennessee. There the land is fertile, and farmers practiced a productive, mixed agriculture.[16] Farmers of Grainger and Greene Counties also were limited by inadequate roads, but they could transport their produce to Knoxville by flatboats down the Tennessee River and its tributaries, or by rail over the East Tennessee Railroad, which was completed through Greene County in the late 1850s.[17]

Similarly, the idea that Appalachia was the land of subsistence farmers until recent times is under serious reevaluation. John Inscoe took direct aim at this notion in *Mountain Masters,* a study of slavery in western North Carolina. Inscoe quotes Olive Dame Campbell's observation in 1925 that "there is no fundamental reason for separating mountain people from lowland people, nor are mountain problems so different at bottom from those of other rural areas in the United States," an unusual insight for the time. Inscoe suggests that much the same could be said of antebellum society in the southern Appalachians generally.[18] On the eve of the Civil War, Inscoe argues, "western North Carolina was far from the backward, isolated area it was later seen to be." In fact, "the variety of situations and the diversity of its populace equaled if not surpassed those of any other rural section of the antebellum South." Furthermore, although the Carolina mountains retained some of the "crude aspects of its frontier origins," the area "constituted a thriving, productive, and even a progressive society."[19]

Scholars of the 1960s broke with the established school of historical approach which focused on universal themes that thread their way through American history, binding the nation together, and became much more interested in the diversity of the American experience. More recently, this shift in focus found expression in Appalachian history as well. The "new" social history, as it was called, has exerted more influence on Appalachian studies than any other branch of history by challenging many of the assumptions (and shibboleths) of American history. One of these challenges in particular, that individualism and capitalism provided the economic foundation of America from earliest colonial origins, is a debate that promises to rewrite what has passed for Appalachian history. Another debate involves the nature of community culture in early America: Was it essentially cooperative or competitive? Were colonial farmers a self-sufficient, precapitalist people who emphasized community harmony over personal self-interest, or were they commercially aggressive, market-oriented, profit-maximizers? In short, were communal farmers initially "modernized" by capitalism into competitive economic men and women, or was capitalism part of their culture from the beginning?[20] Ideology, of course, provided the motive power behind this debate.

Scholars who apply this approach to mountain life are rapidly changing our historical perspective on the relationship of community to market development in preindustrial Appalachia. Historical geographer Robert D. Mitchell's study of frontier Virginia rejects the self-sufficiency thesis. He argues instead that settlers moving west were motivated by economic profit from the beginning.[21]

Robert McKenzie's study of Tennessee directly refutes the oft-repeated view of Ronald D. Eller that in preindustrial Appalachia mountaineers owned their own farms, worked the land as a family unit, and employed a strategy of household self-sufficiency that allowed them to avoid reliance on the market economy. Until the industrial transition at the turn of the twentieth century, "few areas of the United States more closely exemplified Thomas Jefferson's vision of a democratic society."[22] McKenzie contends that the isolation of northeastern Tennessee farmers from the markets meant that they were indeed "self-sufficient," but self-sufficiency meant a "precarious" existence at best. He rejects the idea that hardship was offset by the benefits of communal support, strong kinship networks, and particularly, economic independence. While there were social and cultural costs associated with market involvement, he contends that "it is important also not to lose sight of the undeniable economic costs of persistent market isolation."[23] The income disparity among individual farming households in the mountain counties, McKenzie found, "stemmed not from difference in land tenure or slave ownership but in commercial orientation."[24] In any event, self-sufficiency was not inconsistent with production for exchange, and most farmers engaged in both modes of production. Indeed, only those with the smallest farms did not produce anything for exchange. It was neither an aversion to risk nor an indifference to wealth accumulation that discouraged a commercial orientation among them, but rather high transportation costs, low commodity prices, declining soil fertility, and above all, the declining size of farms. McKenzie concludes that agricultural historian Morton Rothstein is correct in observing that self-sufficiency is merely a "delightful euphemism for rural poverty."[25]

Certainly there were isolated sections of Appalachia, such as Beech Creek, Kentucky, where Brown and Schwarzweller, and Billings, Blee, and Swanson have shown that residents continued to rely on household production until well into the twentieth century.[26] Paul Salstrom turns the issue upside down in his book, *Appalachia's Path to Dependency,* contending that, instead of self-sufficiency losing ground to the entrepreneurial ideology, Appalachia followed the reverse pattern. According to Salstrom, declining agricultural production was the primary reason for Appalachia's shift from market production in the 1840s to a subsistence, producer-consumer system as a way to survive under increasingly marginalized economic circumstances—a reversal of the process as it is commonly understood.[27]

Studies of Appalachia that do not attack the self-sufficiency thesis directly have demonstrated by strong implication that a commercial orientation developed early in sections of the region suitable to market production. A wide variety of economic activities have been documented in Appalachia, taking us far beyond the marginal hard-scrabble hill farm stereotype. By far the most significant of these economically and historically was the livestock business. During the antebellum era, Appalachia was the livestock-raising center of the eastern United States. Most recently, Richard MacMaster examined the early cattle industry in western Virginia and found that from the colonial era forward backcountry stock raisers were "remarkable" in their receptivity to new methods, improved breeding stock, and scientific agriculture in a way that most planters were not. They originated the feeder-lot-system, were among the first to import pedigreed cattle, and played a major role in the diffusion of the beef cattle industry beyond the Appalachians into Kentucky and Ohio.[28]

Stock raising played a significant role in the upper Shenandoah Valley and Potomac highlands of western Virginia. The South Branch valley was known for its cattle as early as the 1750s, and by the 1780s was a major center for cattle raising and feeding for export to eastern markets. In fact, the modern feeder-lot system has its earliest developmental roots in western Virginia, having evolved in the South Branch of the Potomac River and the Greenbrier River valleys. Cattle from Ohio were sent here to be fattened up for the final leg of the drive to eastern cities. In the 1850s shipment by train took the place of driving, and feeders tracked market prices in order to time the arrival of their stock in the markets at the most advantageous moment. Towns and even small cities grew around the trade as gathering centers developed where local producers could sell their cattle to professional drovers. Lewisburg in Greenbrier County, West Virginia, for example, was one local node in a distribution network that pointed livestock toward the regional center of Covington, Virginia, from which they were shipped by rail to Richmond as early as the 1850s. Winchester, in the Shenandoah Valley, became the regional shipping center for stockmen of the South Branch.[29]

John Inscoe demonstrated that at the southern end of the Great Appalachian Valley in North Carolina "livestock production was the most substantial form of commercial agriculture practiced in the mountains and the primary means of exchange used by merchants and those they dealt with locally and out-of-state." As early as 1800 cattle and hogs were being driven from the Carolina mountains to markets in Charleston, Savannah, Norfolk, and Philadelphia. Although hogs were by far the preferred livestock, cattle, sheep, ducks, and turkeys also were driven over the roads to market. Asheville, located on the Buncombe Turnpike, was the regional center for the western Carolina stock trade, but the traffic significantly increased other related economic activity. Hog drives stimulated corn production among local farmers who also sold their stock to drovers passing on the road. Merchants, innkeepers, and feeding station operators also set up businesses along the pikes to rest and feed the herds and serve the drovers. Inscoe concludes that "most western North Carolinians were involved in this complex trade network" and that "dependence on southern markets was pervasive throughout the mountain counties."[30]

Prominent Appalachian cattlemen were the elites in their world, but most mountain farmers engaged in mixed farming and a range of diverse economic activities in addition to agriculture. Nineteenth-century mountain farmers in eastern Kentucky, for example, spent considerable time hunting and trapping for food and pelts for either the market or to pay taxes. Tyrel Moore found that farm exports from the region included small quantities of ginseng, furs, deer hams, chestnuts, honey, and beeswax. These items were exchanged locally but also exported downstream to the Ohio River valley. Poor roads hindered commercial farming, and many scarce items, such as butter, wool, flax, beeswax, and honey, were produced for home consumption. Cattle and hogs were the preferred livestock and corn the principal grain.[31] Gordon McKinney's study of antebellum western North Carolina leads him to conclude that "the geographic isolation of the North Carolina mountain population was not as great as usually portrayed, and many individuals had substantial dealings with people of the outside world." Even though western North Carolinians attempted to grow much of their own food, they had ceased to be truly self-sufficient by the Civil War at the latest. That they had become dependent on the markets to supply their needs is apparent by the strong demand for finished goods and the suffering that they endured from war-inflated prices.[32]

Economic diversification grew hand in hand with a much greater degree of social stratification than the myth of Appalachia would allow. New studies show that almost from the beginning mountain settlements spawned a commercial elite, and subsequent population growth and the adoption of slavery ensured that mountain society would not only be class-differentiated but heterogeneous as well. Also, it is becoming increasingly clear that different sections of the mountains followed different development patterns. In fact, even within the same county significant variations in social and economic relationships often coexisted. A small but influential middle class of doctors, lawyers, merchants, and politicians who served preindustrial mountain communities were directly linked to, and served as mediators with, the broader market economy.[33] Access to land, however, was the key ingredient to the formation of social stratification in preindustrial Appalachia. Scholarship on this issue has only just begun for Appalachia, but we have much to learn from studies of older settled regions, such as early New England and the Mid-Atlantic colonies. Studies of the western Virginia backcountry during the eighteenth century by McClesky, Hughes, Hofstra, and Rasmussen demonstrate that the best lands were engrossed by a small interrelated elite who either operated on their own or acted as agents for wealthy clients.[34] The acquisition of ever larger landholdings by small select groups continued during the nineteenth century. Mary Beth Pudup's study of antebellum southeastern Kentucky revealed the extent to which land-ownership was one of the key factors in the emergent social stratification in these counties as early as the 1820s. Kinship also was important in facilitating the acquisition of lands by providing another vital strand in the political and economic web that bound together local elites.[35] Robert McKenzie found similar evidence for social stratification in the mountains of Tennessee. On the eve of the Civil War, Tennessee's mountain counties were characterized by a great concentration of wealth, extensive landlessness (42.5 percent average), and great income disparity between a minority of farmers who produced for the market and a poor majority who did not.[36] A similar conclusion was reached by Ralph Mann in his work on four farm communities in Tazewell County, Virginia, between 1820 and 1850. The social structure of these communities confirms Pudup's thesis that the control of local resources and the ability to respond to changes maintained the dominant, and usually earliest, landowning native elite families in a position to retain economic control and political power.[37] The economic stratification suggested in the new studies underscores the dangers of facile generalizations about preindustrial mountain communities and challenges the notion of Appalachia as a Jeffersonian Eden.

It is easy to forget that manufactures related to agriculture served a vital function in the early mountain economy, particularly gristmills, wool-carding mills, sawmills, and tanyards, which grew in relationship to the density of settlement and social complexity that evolved over time. Natural resource industries, although secondary to farming as a means of securing a livelihood in preindustrial Appalachia, also employed an increasing number of people throughout the nineteenth century. It was natural for mountaineers to harvest the forest around them for profit. From the earliest settlement they had used the timber to construct dwellings, barns and outbuildings, mills, and other necessary structures. As demand for wood products increased with the population in the mountains and beyond, timber became a market commodity. From the antebellum era to the end of the nineteenth century, mountain rivers were choked in the spring with rafts of logs heading downstream to the mills. They sent more than raw sawlogs to downstream markets, however, as illustrated in the report of the chief engineer for just one lock and dam on the Little Kanawha River in West Virginia for the period between 1876 and 1877: 388 rafts of logs; 1,162,900 feet of sawed lumber; 3,406,200 oil-barrel staves; 57,749 railroad ties; 343,000 hoop-poles; 45,050 cubic feet of ship timber. Except for the staves, these products were exported to Ohio, New York, Pennsylvania, Maryland, and England.[38]

Salt and iron were among the first industries to develop in the mountains, and both contributed to the development of a nascent coal industry in central Appalachia. The Kanawha Valley of western Virginia became a major supplier of salt for the Ohio River cities and even farther downstream to New Orleans for export. For a half-century after its founding in the early nineteenth century, the salt industry grew and stimulated local development of coal to fire the salt brine boilers, and after the Civil War when the salt industry declined, a vital coal industry took its place as a major employer.[39] Throughout the mountains local blacksmiths plied their trade, but in areas where suitable iron ores were found, the iron industry thrived. During the earliest period charcoal provided the primary fuel for iron furnaces, and a plentiful supply of wood was readily available in the mountains. The charcoal iron industry grew to major proportions in western Maryland, western Virginia, and eastern Tennessee, but charcoal furnaces smelted iron for local markets throughout Appalachia. By the mid-nineteenth century, technology permitted the use of coal to fire iron furnaces. Consequently, the proximity of coal and iron deposits provided the points of concentration for the industry in the mountains, especially in the Cumberland River basin of Tennessee, southeastern Pennsylvania, and northwestern Virginia.[40]

Historians now find a much more politically diversified region as well. Gordon McKinney's study of Appalachian politics from the Civil War to 1900 demonstrates that a significant number of residents in certain sections of the mountains, such as eastern Tennessee, northwestern Virginia, and eastern Kentucky were Unionists in their sympathies.[41] By no means, however, did mountaineers represent a Unionist dagger pointed at the heart of the Confederacy. John Inscoe's study of western North Carolina revises the popular notion that Appalachia was a Union bastion filled with freedom-loving frontiersmen. Indeed, 90 percent of western North Carolinians were not slave owners, and they had waged a protracted and sometimes bitter political struggle with eastern elites. But in the end they marched off in record numbers to join the Confederate armies because they identified themselves as southerners, and their economic interests, forged by the traditionally strong trade ties with Georgia and South Carolina, were tied to the South.[42]

It was the development of trade ties that prompted Southwest Virginia to follow Richmond out of the Union and into the Confederacy, a process that ultimately led to the rending of Virginia and the creation of loyal West Virginia. Kenneth Noe shows how the Virginia and Tennessee Railroad, completed between Richmond and Southwest Virginia in the 1850s, linked the economic fortunes of the mountain section with the eastern tidewater capital of Richmond. The creation of West Virginia, which abolished slavery and forged close commercial ties with the northern markets by trade over the Baltimore and Ohio Railroad as well as by river and road, demonstrates the divisiveness of secession politics in the mountain sections of the slave states.[43] The dismemberment of Virginia also reemphasizes the importance of understanding the history of economic development in the mountains, which often is assumed to have begun only with the industrial transition at the turn of the twentieth century.

The reason northwestern Virginia counties remained with the Union and the southwestern counties followed Richmond into the Confederacy is part of a much larger set of issues, but clearly secession sympathies were directly linked to economic dependencies. Noe states that the commercially-minded in Richmond "unloaded their ideology as well as their goods off the train. Not only did southern modernization and slavery go hand in hand, but the determination to defend slavery and the broader economic and social system it held on its back joined them. . . . The leading factor convincing most southwestern Virginians to don gray and most northwestern Virginians blue in 1861 was the divergence among western Virginians caused by their railroads; where they ran and what they carried, and how economic change caused by railroad building shaped ideology."[44]

There were few slaveholders in western Virginia, but the southwestern and northwestern counties split over the issue of secession from the Union, demonstrating some fundamental differences in the political economy of the mountain districts. Van Beck Hall's study of politics in Appalachian Virginia between 1790 and 1830 documents just how early, vigorous, and universal the push for economic development was at least within some sections of the region. By analyzing voting patterns on key economic development issues in the Virginia Assembly and at state conventions, Hall found that settlers in Appalachian Virginia were more diversified, less fearful of change, and more inclined to use government to accomplish development than were "the more cosmopolitan, longer-settled residents of Virginia counties east of the Blue Ridge."[45]

A cursory examination of western Virginia even during this early period reveals the folly of thinking about the region in simplistic terms even for its early years. Most rural settlements had their own grain mills, tanneries, salt, and iron manufacture. Along with the settlements, numerous small towns and resorts along the Allegheny Front provided local markets for farmers throughout the nineteenth century.

Larger towns dotted the western landscape. In fact, Wheeling, Martinsburg, Harpers Ferry, and Wellsburg in present West Virginia were among the fifteen largest towns in the state and represented an evolving urban-commercializing process that increased the political influence of merchants and professionals and the growth of social institutions associated with urban life.[46]

"The growth of these towns created two Appalachias," Hall contends, one composed of counties with growth centers and another made up of rural farm counties, often referred to as "back counties." The counties with growing towns spearheaded the economic diversification of Appalachian Virginia, while the counties without towns failed to develop much commercialization or diversity, according to Hall. Significant differences existed within the western counties, of course, with the residents of towns and more developed counties leading the campaign for economic development and political reform. Westerners stood as one in demands for economic development measures, especially bank charters. But it was the battle over internal improvements that indicates most clearly the economic orientation of western Virginians. Westerners, both rural and urban, almost unanimously supported improvements in transportation. They supported improving navigation of the Potomac in 1795 and constructing a bridge over the Cheat River in 1805, and they backed the James River and Kanawha Canal improvements from 1816 on. Likewise, western support for the improvement and construction of existing roads and turnpikes was nearly unanimous, with little difference between rural and urban counties.[47]

According to Hall, historians have failed to recognize that supposedly backward Appalachian residents "actually backed democratization, the involvement of more individuals in the political process, banks, internal improvements, the protection of the flow of capital and credit, and education and occasionally challenged the institution of slavery." In fact, even the subsistence farmers of the underdeveloped counties voted for programs that many historians associated with progress and modernization. "These actions simply cannot be fitted into the usual portrayal of an Appalachia trapped in a sort of late eighteenth or early nineteenth-century 'time warp' or of a culture and society that was easily manipulated by powerful outside interests," Hall argues. What popular and scholarly writers alike have failed to appreciate, Hall concludes, is that in western Virginia,

---

Two Appalachias existed side by side. The one with towns, newspapers, banks, and early industries already differed from the more rural, isolated, farming counties. These counties, much easier to identify with the traditional picture of Appalachia, were less interested in many of the programs backed by their more urbanized colleagues, but even those who lived in the second Appalachia worked much harder for reform and development than did the supposedly more commercial, involved, and aware residents of eastern Virginia. The traditional picture of isolated mountain folk uninterested or uninvolved in outside political questions did not yet exist by 1830.[48]

It is noteworthy that, at the height of local color writing and the reification of the myth of Appalachia, strategic sections of the region were in the throes of a wrenching industrial transition. No section of the mountains was affected by this process more dramatically than central Appalachia. Industrial society advanced into the mountains behind armies of resident and imported laborers who laid the tracks for three major railroad systems. The first to cut its way through the plateau was the Chesapeake and Ohio Railroad, fulfilling a dream dating back to the eighteenth century, when planners of the C and O Canal hoped to connect Virginia tidewater ports with the Ohio River. Armies of laborers invaded the formerly inaccessible New River Gorge country laying the iron rails that would bind Richmond and Huntington in 1873.[49]

The Pocahontas and Flat Top coalfields of West Virginia, southwest of the C and O line, were connected to the national markets by the Norfolk and Western Railroad. This company was organized in 1881 specifically to serve as a coal carrier linking the southern West Virginia and southwestern Virginia coal country with the port of Norfolk and eventually the Great Lakes. The N and W offered financial assistance to investors for the construction of mines and towns along its right-or-way, and in 1883 when the railroad reached Pocahontas, Virginia, on the West Virginia line, the town was already in full operation with large stockpiles of coal ready for immediate shipment. Eventually, the N and W built a major branch line to Big Stone Gap in Wise County, Virginia, and forged ahead with the main line along the Guyandotte River Valley to the Ohio River, and on to the Great Lakes.[50]

While the C and O and the N and W were developing central Appalachia from the east, the Louisville and Nashville Railroad began constructing lines into the Kentucky coalfields from the west. The main line passed along the edge of the plateau running from Louisville to Knoxville. Determined to dominate the eastern Kentucky fields, the L and N constructed a branch line from Corbin, Kentucky, to the Cumberland Gap in the 1880s, but the Kentucky River highlands were not reached by rail until the eve of World War I, when the L and N branch line was completed into Harlan, Letcher, and Perry Counties.[51] Eventually, the entire region was integrated into an elaborate network of main lines, branch lines, feeder lines, and spurs for transporting natural resources extracted from the central Appalachian countryside.

In the southern Appalachians the boom came to the western North Carolina and eastern Tennessee regions with the arrival of the Western North Carolina Railroad at Asheville in 1880 and at the Tennessee state line in 1882. Asheville became a boomtown, and the pioneer developers soon gave way to the large companies, often with operations in several states as the industry was consolidated during the first decade of the twentieth century.[52] Because of its strategic location within the southern mountain region, Knoxville had been an evolving commercial and transportation hub for nearly a century when the convergence of railroads and Cumberland coal and iron elevated the city to the status of regional development hub. From this growth center commercial and modernizing influences reached out into the surrounding mountains. Because Knoxville's coal and iron became locked into a supporting role to the Birmingham coal-steel complex by United States Steel Corporation, and because the city was a major railroad hub, Knoxville's primary industry became light manufacturing, which drew on the surrounding mountain population for its labor force, rather than the black "industrial reserve" of the Black Belt.[53]

The tri-cities of Elizabethtown, Bristol, and Johnson City, Tennessee, held a similar strategic position on the emerging railroad system in the mountains, and they, too, went through a period of development. The tri-cities' industrial expansion attracted immigrants and blacks, but most of them worked in construction and extractive industries. The subsequent development of the tri-cities as a textile manufacturing center provided work primarily for white people in the surrounding countryside, following the southern pattern of a "dual economy" whereby blacks worked in the cotton fields and poor whites worked in the mills.[54]

The enormous capital investment poured into central Appalachian railroads, timber, and coal mining completed the social and economic transition of the region. Trains carried away forest products, but they also returned with manufactured goods such as food, dry goods, household furnishings, farm supplies, and whatever else people ordered out of the mail-order catalogs that supplied the needs of town dwellers and farmers. The railroad connected local communities to the national markets and, as elsewhere in rural America, exerted a profound influence on the way people lived. They were the lines of communication that brought in intellectual and material culture in the form of city newspapers, the telegraph, and the telephone along with incoming manufactured goods.

With the circulation of cash and the virtual explosion in the population of wage earners in the mill and mine towns, merchants were increasingly attracted by the potential for trade beyond the towns in the surrounding countryside.[55] Because of the railroad, for example, the county seat town of Logan, West Virginia, had banks, a newspaper, running water, sidewalks, fire hydrants, and a fire department even before there were a single coal mine in the county. Logan was not urban, according to David Corbin, "but the people were neither isolated nor wholly ignorant of industrialization or capitalism. No longer was the area, as a journalist covering the Hatfield-McCoy feud a few years earlier sensationalized, 'as remote as central Africa.'"[56]

Coal operators entering central Appalachia found few of the supporting services required to sustain a workforce, and so the railroads also hauled in the equipment operators required to build their own. The unincorporated company town became one of the defining features of life in the region. Its very nature militated against the development of those civic ideas that became the catechism, if not the practice, of enlightened corporate capitalism elsewhere in America. The company constructed the town's physical plant, became the miners' landlord, provided the police force, built the churches and stores, and provided any other service that the towns required. Of course, there were great differences among company towns, ranging from crude coal camps erected on "gob piles" to model towns with all the modern conveniences and a benevolent owner-operator. All of them, however, were privately owned entities, not sovereign political jurisdictions.[57]

Pioneer industrialists not only had to build their own towns, but a scarcity of labor in the region also necessitated the importation of a workforce. The central Appalachian districts dominated by the coal industry experienced the greatest demand for labor and, therefore, the greatest importation of workers. Consequently, the population of the central Appalachian plateau grew dramatically between 1880 and 1920 from under two hundred thousand in 1870 to over 1.2 million in 1920. However, growth did not proceed uniformly, nor was it evenly distributed. The West Virginia plateau grew rapidly throughout the era, with the population of its southern counties nearly quintupling from 93,174 to 446,051. Kentucky's plateau counties, which already contained a sizable population on the eve of industrialization, grew sporadically from 216,883 to 538,350 during the same period. Virginia's central Appalachian counties, however, grew moderately but steadily from 55,349 to 155,405. The several plateau counties of northern Tennessee contained the smallest population, and over the course of this forty-year period they doubled their population from 45,375 to 96,063.[58]

The preindustrial African American population of central Appalachia was relatively small, totaling only 14,360 in 1870, but by 1890 that figure had more than doubled to 30,226 and quadrupled to 64,251 by 1910. During the decade of World War I, the number of blacks in the region continued to climb, reaching 88,076 by 1920 and 108,872 by 1930 when the immigration ended. Most of this increase was associated with the rise of the coal industry. In 1870 only 36 percent of the African American population of central Appalachia resided in the sixteen major coal-producing counties of the fifty-six-county region. By 1920, however, 96 percent of the blacks living in central Appalachia resided in those sixteen coal counties. By far the greatest increase in the black population came in southern West Virginia, where 69 percent of the region's African Americans (totaling 60,488) and 62 percent of the state's black miners (totaling 17,799) resided by 1920. Here the scope of industrial transformation was greatest and, correspondingly, the demand for labor was strongest as well.[59]

In the coalfields blacks met and mingled with a bewildering array of peoples and cultures. As the immigrants poured into industrializing America during the late nineteenth century, bureaus were established to help deploy (for a fee) the newly arrived laborers to states where employers sought their services. The number of immigrant miners in the region

Table 1 African American Black Population of Central Appalachia, 1880–1990

Year	Kentucky	Tennessee	Virginia	West Virginia	Totals
1880	6,734	2,570	4,242	5,781	19,327
1890	7,444	3,653	6,552	12,577	30,226
1900	7,602	3,609	7,056	21,584	39,851
1910	10,222	4,415	7,669	41,945	64,251
1920	15,692	2,943	8,953	60,488	88,076
1930	18,286	2,129	7,616	80,841	108,872
1940	18,662	1,918	7,709	85,465	113,754
1950	14,284	2,941	6,659	86,421	110,305
1960	10,240	2,884	4,083	64,613	81,820
1970	7,232	2,718	2,585	44,956	57,491
1980	6,506	3,253	2,688	42,277	54,724
1990	5,602	3,413	2,446	35,004	46,465

Source: U.S. Bureau of the Census, Characteristics of the Population for the decennial censuses 1880 through and including 1990.
Note: Counties included within the central Appalachian subregion: (Kentucky) Bell, Breathitt, Carter, Clay, Elliott, Estill, Floyd, Harlan, Jackson, Johnson, Knott, Knox, Laurel, Lawrence, Lee, Leslie, Letcher, Magoffin, Martin, Menifee, Morgan, Owsley, Perry, Pike, Powell, Rockcastle, Rowan, Wayne, Wolfe, and Whitley; (Tennessee) Anderson, Campbell, Claiborne, Morgan, and Scott; (Virginia) Buchanan, Dickenson, Lee, Russell, Tazewell, and Wise; (West Virginia) Boone, Braxton, Clay, Fayette, Kanawha, Lincoln, Logan, McDowell, Mercer, Mingo, Nicholas, Raleigh, Summers, Webster, and Wyoming.

grew dramatically between 1880 and 1920. Although there are no precise estimates for central Appalachia, the number of immigrants must have reached at least one-quarter of the mine workforce, and in some locations, much higher. In West Virginia, the number of foreign miners among the mine labor force was less than one thousand in 1870. By 1907 their number had reached nearly sixteen thousand, and on the eve of World War I (1915), after the flow of new immigrants had stopped and at least half of the immigrants had returned to their native lands, immigrant coal miners in West Virginia still totaled almost thirty-two thousand. These immigrants, representing nearly all of the nations of Europe, came to the Appalachian coalfields in much the same manner that immigrants came to other areas of America during this period. Some were deployed from Ellis Island by labor agents who worked the port towns as representatives of either states or companies. Many followed the typical chain migration pattern whereby family and friends established a "beachhead" for others from the region who joined them later.[60]

In the coalfields, native whites, African Americans, and foreign immigrants lived and worked in company towns where they usually were segregated into sections designated as "Colored Town," "Hunky Hollow," or "Little Italy." Generally, there was discrimination in the kinds of jobs available to each group in the mine as well, with natives or British immigrants serving as bosses or in the technical positions, and blacks and immigrants in the harder, more dangerous, and most unsteady jobs. Still, blacks and immigrants were attracted by relatively high wages. Underground the men worked together, but even on the surface the rigid segregation often became blurred in company towns, and without other employment opportunities, the workers came to focus on their common economic interests in the United Mine Workers of America, the one organization in the coalfields they could control.[61]

Table 2 Race and Ethnic Origins of West Virginia Coal Miners by County, 1909

	Fayette	Raleigh	Mercer	McDowell	Totals
Mines Reporting	96	24	17	70	207
Native/White	5,724	1,062	907	3,217	10,910
Black	2,949	455	927	4,419	8,750
Italian	978	137	398	1,648	3,161
Hungarian	392	83	227	1,056	1,758
Polish	319	67	42	179	607
Lithuanian	46	10	—	5	61
Swedish	9	2	—	20	31
English	122	26	7	21	176
Austrian	70	3	—	10	83
Russian	77	30	17	416	540
German	108	15	6	36	165
Scottish	93	15	—	4	112
Litvitch	24	12	—	4	40
Greek	5	61	—	130	196
Irish	14	—	—	15	29
Slavish	155	40	33	401	629
Syrian	15	—	—	—	15
Romanian	9	—	—	120	129
Unknown/Other	1,750	801	369	2,894	5,814
Totals	12,859	2,819	2,933	14,595	33,202

Source: West Virginia Department of Mines, Report of the Chief Inspector (Charleston, 1909), 94–95.
Note: The number of blacks and Hungarians would be considerably larger if figures for the Virginia portion of the Pocahontas field were available, because one of the largest employers of black and Hungarian miners in the field was located just across the state line.

Industrializing Appalachia was a matrix of cultural interaction among very diverse races and cultures. Coal operators sought a "judicious mixture" of native whites, blacks, and foreign immigrants to balance the dissonant cultural traits that were seen as weaknesses by the operators. Like workers elsewhere in America before work was mechanized and control was shifted to the owners of production, mountaineers tended to take time off from work for hunting and fishing, planting, harvesting, family reunions, weddings, and other family affairs. Recognizing "blue Monday" by staying in bed after a weekend drinking bout was common throughout industrializing America.[62] Most immigrants in the coalfields were from southern and eastern Europe, and their Catholicism itself provided striking contrast to the austere Protestantism found among most of the indigenous residents. One Catholic priest observed of the southwestern Virginia coalfields around Norton in the 1920s: "As to the nationalities that make up the vast congregation at present . . . there are only four American born families in the whole section; Roda is all Hungarian, Inman half Hungarian and half Slavs, in the other camps the Catholics are about evenly divided between Poles and Slavs . . . and at occasions like First Communion, Confirmation or dedication of a new church, the outpouring of Catholics is quite a revelation and one would imagine to live for the time in a village of the former Austrian-Hungarian Empire."[63] The extent of cultural exchange and eventually intermarriage among this extremely heterogeneous population usually is unappreciated even by regional scholars. All of these groups carried their own cultural traditions with them into the mountains and influenced others by their presence.

The transition to industry in central Appalachia produced the most dramatic example of development of racial and ethnic diversity within the region, but we should not lose sight of the fact that African Americans and the racially mixed Melungeons had resided in southern Appalachia since the earliest settlement days, and Native Americans from time immemorial.[64]

Until recently, writers have accepted the longstanding assumption that, because of geographical isolation, rural Appalachia had functioned in the past as a subculture that was essentially autonomous from mainstream society. Accordingly, its culture was regulated by traditional values they associated with the frontier, such as traditionalism, individualism, familism, and fundamentalism. Many believed that Appalachia's traditional values, insulated by geographic and cultural isolation, were barriers that explained the "backward" economy found in the mountains and sustained by a "culture of poverty."

The belief in a distinct, regionwide Appalachian subculture resistant to economic development was shaped by a large body of literature that accepted uncritically a fictional Appalachia invented by local color writers of the late nineteenth century. A review of this literature, however, reveals remarkably little empirical evidence for the proposition that Appalachian culture was the product of continuing frontier isolation. Recent historical research challenges the fictional Appalachia by demonstrating that, when viewed from the perspective of the preindustrial era, Appalachia was not much different from other regions of nineteenth-century rural America. Therefore, the pervasive assumption that modern economic problems in the region somehow stem from Appalachia's long physical and cultural isolation must be reconsidered.

CHAPTER 20

Work, Poverty, and Health in Appalachia

by Richard A. Couto, Phillip J. Obermiller, and Julia C. DeBruicker

The "obvious" connection of socio-economic status and health may be more elusive than at first glance. This article suggests two related intervening links between poverty and health: the nature of local work opportunities and the place of women in the labor force. Using county-level data from the last four census reports, it indicates that high rates of women's labor force participation in areas with low participation, among all adults, signal the most severe forms of Appalachian poverty. Those same areas have significantly higher rates of childhood mortality; mortality rates and health risk behaviors of the working age population; and higher risks for chronic illness among the elderly. Thus, the nature of work force opportunities and the place of women within them may be keys to explaining some chronic illness disparities within the region. The article summarizes the 2004 Ford Foundation-funded special issue of the *Journal of Appalachian Studies* to explain the geographic definitions of Appalachia, its subregions, and the spatial distribution of work opportunities and health status within the region.

> *Social epidemiology* explicitly investigates social determinants of population distributions of health, disease, and well-being, rather than treating such determinants as mere background to biomedical phenomena. Social epidemiology uses an attention to theories, concepts and methods conducive to illuminating intimate links between our bodies and the body politic.[26]

POVERTY AND HEALTH IN GENERAL

In 1993, the editors of a volume on Appalachian community-based initiatives on cancer prevention sought a chapter on the relationship of socio-economic status and cancer. That chapter proved elusive. Reports on the "obvious" relationship of poverty and cancer and other forms of illness had a taken-for-granted nature that cited the same non-empirical sources. Rigorous research that tested those assumptions indicated far more complicated relationships than simply, poor people are sicker. For example, higher socioeconomic status may be associated with higher incidence of some illnesses, such as skin cancer. In the case of breast cancers, rates of incidence also increase with socio-economic status but mortality rates decline because increases in socio-economic status mean increased access to screening and early detection.[1]

Since then, social epidemiology has probed the correlations of poverty and health and the complicated nature of that relationship.[2] An extensive 1988 British government study showed, unexpectedly, that social and economic differences coincided with differences in health status among people at every rung of the socio-economic ladder. Not only were poor people sicker than well-to-do people but those better off among the well-to-do reported better health than those less well-to-do.[3] With that finding in mind, subsequent investigators searched for the nature and extent of the more complex effect of social and economic differences on health care and health status.[4]

Researchers began to examine *how* social factors and illness are related, not *if* they were,

> *Biological expressions of social inequality* refers to how people literally embody and biologically express experiences of economic and social inequality, from in utero to death, thereby producing social inequalities in health across a wide spectrum of outcomes.[27]

and found that the effects of socio-economic status on cardiovascular disease, for one instance, begins in utero, with the behavior and diet of the expectant mother, and continues up to varieties of medical care in old age.[5] Other studies showed that discrimination on the basis of race and ethnicity, gender, sexual preference, age, disability, and class led to higher than average incidences of infant mortality;

> *Discrimination*—the process by which a member, or members, or a socially defined group is, or are, treated differently (especially unfairly) because of his/her/their membership in that group.[28]

higher age-adjusted mortality rates; fewer years of healthy life; higher rates of violence and abuse; higher rates of smoking and substance abuse; and higher rates of denial of health insurance.[6] These socio-economic determinants also influence risky health behaviors and self-reported conditions of health.[7]

The research on the association of social and economic disparities with health status revealed anomalies to the simple explanations of income differences and wealth. There was no gradient of inequality and health status among nations such as those found among income groups in Britain. Instead, some low-income nations had higher life expectancies than other nations with greater wealth. Portugal, for example, with half the per capita gross domestic product of the United States had about the same life expectancy.[8] Further study showed that social conditions *within* nations seemed to explain the differences of health status *among* nations. Nations with little wealth but equitable distributions of wealth, Cuba and Costa Rica for example, had higher or equal life expectancy rates than nations with far more wealth.[8,9] Apparently, the size of the economic pie is less important to health status than how the pie is sliced and shared.

POVERTY AND HEALTH IN APPALACHIA

Attention to unhealthy socio-economic disparity raises a public health challenge for the United States and its poorest regions, one of which is Appalachia. The rest of the country uses "Appalachia" as a standard of poverty, just as "barrio," "reservation," and "inner city." We might expect that given how the pie of American prosperity is sliced and the portion that Appalachia shares we would find health disparities between the nation and the region. We would be right.

The most comprehensive and thorough examination of Appalachian health disparities found that the region had higher age-adjusted rates of mortality for all persons 35 to 64 than the nation on several causes of death: all cancers—particularly lung, breast, colorectal; diabetes; heart disease; stroke; chronic obstructive pulmonary disease (COPD); motor vehicle accidents; and accidental deaths. The region had far higher infant mortality rates than the rest of the nation as well. As might be expected, these rates varied within the region by gender and race; less expected, they also varied considerably by subregion with the most extreme rates in the Central Appalachia coal counties.[10]

Evidently, not all parts of Appalachia are "Appalachian." Indeed, the Appalachian region varies dramatically.[11] About two-thirds of the Appalachian counties are rural but the region has metropolitan counties as well, with modest size cities, and large urban areas such as Knoxville, Chattanooga, Pittsburgh, and Birmingham. The 410 Appalachian counties incorporate the entire state of West Virginia and portions of 12 other states in a corridor running from 1 to 7 o'clock from New York to Mississippi, Alabama, and Georgia. Thus, some Appalachian counties adjoin major metropolitan areas including Atlanta, Cincinnati, Harrisburg, Lexington, Memphis, and Montgomery. Obviously, we have a rural-metropolitan distinction within the region that parallels the rural, suburban, and urban distinctions of the nation.

Subregions add other intra-regional distinctions. Northern Appalachia includes counties in New York, Pennsylvania, Maryland, Ohio and most of West Virginia; Central Appalachia takes in all of the Kentucky Appalachian counties and contiguous counties in Tennessee, Virginia, and West Virginia; and Southern Appalachia incorporates the remaining counties in Tennessee and Virginia and all the Appalachian counties in North Carolina, South Carolina, Georgia, Alabama, and Mississippi. Subsequently, we now have rural, urban, and metropolitan counties in three subregions.

The census of the general population permits us to measure how Appalachia compares with the rest of the nation. The 2000 census data for the region were analyzed in a special issue of the *Journal of Appalachian Studies*[12] including analyses of the region's age structure, sex and gender dynamics, ethnic and racial diversity, educational attainment, labor force participation, income and poverty distributions, migration patterns, household formation, and housing patterns.[13;14;15;16;17;18;19;20;21]

The measures of 2000 show intra-regional and other spatial differences within Appalachia that concern us here. The Southern subregion has more people, better income, and less poverty than the other two regions. The rural counties of all the subregions have less of these than the metropolitan counties, however.[11;22]

Northern and Southern Appalachia have reversed places since 1970 on measures of income, population, and employment. Central Appalachia, the place of poverty in the United States consciousness, has remained an economically depressed region. In 1969, the per capita personal income of the entire Appalachian region was 79.5 percent of the national figure. In 1999, the region was at 81 percent; a modest but positive increase. During that same period of time, Northern Appalachia's share dropped from 86.6 to 83.9 percent and Southern Appalachia's share increased from 74.7 to 84.7 percent. Central Appalachia's share started at 57.7 and enjoyed a spike related to the coal boom of the 1970s before coming down to 65 percent.[11, p. 249]

The persistent poverty of Central Appalachia, the shifting fortunes of Northern and Southern Appalachia, and the lag of rural counties compared with metropolitan over time seem to have roots in the market economy for labor. In simplest terms, Appalachia offers a microcosm of broad national and international economic changes. Manufacturing production has shifted from old sites to new ones; from an organized labor force to unorganized; and from a decline in labor intense modes of production relative to capital intense ones. The upshot of these economic changes is a migration of high-paying manufacturing jobs from the north and central subregions to the south and the occurrence of new employment opportunities in capital and other services in the south.[17;19]

There are social consequences to these economic and technological changes. Regression analysis using civilian labor force participation yields significant positive correlations for population change and per capita income. They yield significant negative correlations for the portion of children in the population, the rate of childhood poverty, and the overall rate of poverty.[23]

The highest correlations are found in the comparison of the rate of civilian labor force participation and the portion of women in the civilian labor force. As the women worker per work opportunity ratio goes up, the fortunes of workers and the economic security of their families decline.[23] These strong negative correlations suggest that women enter the secondary and tertiary labor force of limited opportunity for low-wage work in higher rates than their entry into the primary labor force. For example, with the decline in coal industry employment, a primary labor market with high pay and benefits and appeal to the most qualified males of working age, shrinks. Wage earners, especially males, will seek other primary labor markets within commuting or migration distance. The labor force left behind will have fewer opportunities for full-time, well-paying jobs with benefits. These may be temporary jobs for some workers who have momentarily lost work in the primary labor market or those who are preparing to join it, for example students. The tertiary labor force, however, are workers who are place-bound, such as female family heads, disabled, ethnic minorities, elderly, and less qualified, by education, training, or experience, than other workers. For them, there is no alternative but to work at part-time, high-turnover, low-paying, and temporary jobs.

The portion of women in the civilian labor force, itself an indicator of secondary and tertiary labor forces, correlates strongly with measures of poverty. Unlike other measures of civilian labor force participation however, the measures of women in the civilian labor force correlate positively with the portion of children in the population, the rate of childhood poverty, and the overall rate of poverty, and negatively with population increase and per capita income.

The persistent poverty of Central Appalachia and the change in fortunes of Northern and Southern Appalachia may be the price that people pay for defying the market's allocation of labor or for their inability or unwillingness to leave a place where their labor is not valued. This price falls heaviest on children and women who subsidize the unmitigated portion of market economics in Appalachia and those other places of low opportunities for work—barrios, reservations, and inner-cities.

WORK, POVERTY, AND HEALTH IN APPALACHIA

These findings on work and poverty coincide with findings on poverty and health care in terms of geographic space. The greatest disparities in health outcomes and healthcare may be found in the coalmining counties of Central Appalachia and rural counties in Southern Appalachia, especially those with large African-American populations; exactly where the most severe rates of poverty and the disproportionate female participation in the civilian labor force may be found. Recent studies have found differences in health status and behavior for working age adults, children, and seniors.

Working Age Adults: A recent study of health disparities in Appalachia found "considerable variability" among rates of mortality in the Appalachian region. The central region is most frequently represented by high rates of hospitalization for any cause as well as primary diagnoses including heart disease, lung cancer, COPD, and diabetes." Central Appalachia similarly sees the greatest prevalence of adverse health behaviors, such as sedentary lifestyles and tobacco use.[10] Low educational attainment, a characteristic of secondary and tertiary labor markets, and older age status are also associated with higher rates of tobacco use, which account in part for the high rates of smoking in the region and high cancer mortality rates in rural Appalachian counties.[24]

Children: As civilian labor force participation declines because of a lack of employment opportunities the portion of children in poverty increases and at even higher rates where women make up a large portion of the work force.[23] In Central Appalachia, one in three children, under six years of age, lives in poverty, while in the Northern and Southern subregions the prevalence is closer to one in five.[18] Poverty influences children's nutrition and thus their physiological ability to grow and learn. A report on rural children suggests that the larger rate of mortality among children 1 to 4–42 per 100,000 compared with 30 for urban children—"are linked to the higher poverty rates, lower education levels, lack of prenatal care specialists practicing in rural areas, and frequent deaths by automobile and all-terrain vehicle accidents."[25]

Seniors: The population over 65 years of age does not vary significantly with the variation in total labor force participation; probably because government policies of Social Security and Medicare mitigate the worst consequences of poverty for those over 65 and out of the labor force. However, as the working age population declines in places of declining labor markets, Northern and Central Appalachia are aging more rapidly than the balance of the nation.[13] Obviously, an aging population has greater need for geriatric medicine, access to pharmaceuticals, long-term care, and treatment facilities for chronic diseases. Older Appalachian residents have lower educational attainment measures and higher degrees of illiteracy. This leads to special problems with health education programs, the comprehension of diagnoses, and compliance with treatment.

CONCLUSION

The health disparities between the Appalachian region and the nation and among the Appalachian subregions invite further social epidemiological work. Labor markets and especially the participation of women in secondary and tertiary labor markets appear to be gross indicators of high risk for chronic illness and health adverse behaviors just as they indicate high degrees of poverty. These poverty and labor force data as well as the health measures recently collected by the Appalachian Regional Commission provide new and important opportunities for detailed social epidemiological studies in the Appalachian region.

CHAPTER 22

Rape of the Appalachians

by Jedediah S. Purdy

Driving his battered sedan through Blair, West Virginia, a cigarette dangling between thin fingers, James Weekley passes among ghosts. "There stood three houses," he says, gesturing at a flat, grassy area below the narrow, two-lane road, "and across the creek were two more. They sold a year back, then they burned." Five years ago, this small town, strung along a creek bottom between two mountains, had stores, an elementary school, and twice the 80 families who now live here. Then the Dal-Tex coal company began strip-mining Blair Mountain. Since then, the community has been darkened by dust storms, battered by flying rock, and shaken by dynamite blasts. Every month more residents sell their homes to the company and move out. When the job is done, not much will be left of the town or the mountain.

Coal mining is an old story in Appalachia, but Blair has been claimed by a new kind of boom. Today's mining is driven by mountaintop removal, a method of strip-mining that does just what the name suggests. On a mountaintop mine, a company blasts and bulldozes hundreds of vertical feet from a cluster of connected peaks, turning them into a single field of pulverized rock. The bulldozers push millions of tons of earth and stone into the surrounding valleys, filling them hundreds of feet deep. These "valley fills" sometimes run for several miles. Mountains here are small and valleys narrow, and in the wake of a mountaintop mine they blend into a uniform, stony terrain utterly unlike the lush, rugged West Virginian slopes. The hardwood forests of the region do not return to the mine sites. The land mainly supports tough grasses and scrub trees.

Coal companies have strip-mined 500 square miles of West Virginia since 1981, and the pace has increased rapidly. In the past three years, the state's Division of Environmental Protection (DEP) has authorized 27,000 acres of new mountaintop mining, after permitting only 9,800 acres throughout the 1980s. The largest existing mine will cover perhaps 20,000 acres before it closes early in the next century, and mines on the same scale are becoming more common. Valley fills have buried 469 miles of streams in five southwestern watersheds and covered an estimated 700 miles of streams across the state.

Most of West Virginia's mountaintop mines are probably illegal. But the DEP has continued to authorize them, with the support of the fed-

Source: Reprinted with permission from *The American Prospect*, Volume 9, Number 41, November 1– December 1, 1998. The American Prospect, 5 Broad Street, Boston, MA 02109. All rights reserved.

eral Office of Surface Mining (OSM). Since Congress passed strip-mining legislation in 1977, state and federal regulation has presented a Rake's Progress of good law gone bad under hostile or indifferent administrations. Meanwhile, no one knows the ecological consequences of pushing tens of thousands of acres of mountains into hundreds of miles of streams. And the strip-miners are not waiting to find out.

THE STRIPPING BOOM

Although almost invisible to the public eye, the coal industry is booming as never before. Coal produces 56 percent of American electricity, and its cost per unit of energy is lower than that of any other fossil fuel. U.S. coal production went over a billion tons for the first time in 1990 and has stayed there in each year since 1994. The average coal miner has tripled his productivity in the past decade.

Those gains come at the cost of wholesale changes in the coal industry. Although dust-coated miners in headlamps still emerge every evening from mines in West Virginia, Kentucky, and Pennsylvania, their numbers have been dwindling for decades. Increasingly they are replaced by bulldozers, explosives, and the Goliaths of the coalfields, earth-moving machines that stand 20 stories high and can pick up 130 tons of dirt and rock with one bite of their shovels. The numbers are striking. Coal employment has declined from 163,000 to 85,000 nationwide in the past decade, and from 29,000 to under 20,000 in West Virginia—down from almost 60,000 20 years ago. In 1948, before the advent of strip-mining, West Virginia alone had more miners than work in the entire nation today.

The heart of the new coal industry is strip-mining and the most efficient form of stripping is mountaintop removal. Strip-mining now accounts for 62 percent of U.S. coal production and one-third of West Virginia's. Nationally, the average stripminer produces three times as much coal as his underground counterpart.

Dropping prices and mounting competition have pushed Appalachia's coal operators toward stripping. The price of coal has fallen steadily from over $30 per ton in 1981 to just over $20 today, thus intensifying the pressure to increase productivity. Western miners have increased their share of national production by more than 10 percent since 1987, benefiting from thick, easily accessible coal seams, and increasing the squeeze on the thin seams and steep mountains of the East. New federal regulations have also increased the value of West Virginia's hard to access coal deposits. The 1990 Clean Air Act mandates that power plants use coal low in sulfur, because high-sulfur coal is the chief cause of acid rain. Southern West Virginia is rich in low-sulfur coal, which is often distributed in thin horizontal veins, like icing in a layer cake, through hundreds of vertical feet of sandstone, earth, and shale. These thin deposits are difficult to mine by traditional methods, but they are ready-made for mountaintop removal.

LAW AND OUTLAWS

Strip-mining in the United States is governed by a 1977 federal law, the Surface Mining Control and Reclamation Act (SMCRA), called "SMACK-ra" by those who work with it. The act was passed after six years of congressional battles and vetoes by President Ford in 1975 and 1976. Its real origins, though, lie in eastern Kentucky, where strip-mining exploded in the 1960s without meaningful regulation, and people whose property lay over coal owned by mining companies found their fields, woods, and family cemeteries destroyed without recompense. (Ownership divided between minerals and surface land has been common in Appalachia since a wave of speculators visited the region at the beginning of this century, buying mineral rights from often illiterate landholders for a tiny fraction of their value.)

In incidents that became folk legends, elderly mountaineers threw themselves to the ground in front of approaching bulldozers, sometimes shaming the strippers into withdrawing. Others broke into the dynamite sheds at stripping sites and used the stolen explosives to sabotage bulldozers and backhoes. At the same time, Kentucky lawyer Harry M. Caudill won national attention with powerful histories of the coal industry's presence in his state, including the bleak, elegiac masterpiece *Night Comes to the Cumberlands*.

By 1972, coalitions of local residents, VISTA staffers fresh from college, and members of the region's nascent environmental movement were agitating across Appalachia for an end to stripping. Then a dam built of mining detritus burst, sending a wall of black water down Buffalo Creek, in Logan County, West Virginia. One hundred and twenty-four people died in the flood. Now no serious person could any longer pretend that a scarred landscape was the only price of stripping.

Strip-mining legislation had already been introduced in Congress by Ken Heckler, a flamboyant, idealistic representative from southern West Virginia. From the beginning, Heckler wanted to ban stripping outright and grant enforcement responsibility to the Environmental Protection Agency (EPA). After the Buffalo Creek disaster, the Nixon administration introduced a weaker bill that would have given states chief responsibility for regulation, overseen by the Bureau of Mines—then widely considered a political arm of the mining industry. Representative Morris Udall of Arizona engineered a compromise that included strong federal standards, allowed strip-mining under restricted conditions, and placed the law in the hands of the new Office of Surface Mining in the Department of Interior. The legislation passed.

Heckler opposed the compromise, warning his colleagues, "You know the economic and political history of this nation. You know the realities of economic and political pressure. You know that neither a State legislature nor any administrative authority can stand up against the wealth and power of a dominant economic group."

Indeed, "King Coal" had long ruled West Virginia politics, with coal companies on the right and the equally imperial United Mine Workers of America (UMWA) on the left. The coal industry owns half of the land in the Appalachian coalfields and as much as 75 percent in West Virginia's top coal-producing counties. In the early 1970s, a study found that every governor and president of the state senate in the previous 20 years had worked in the coal industry before taking office, afterward, or both. Current Governor Cecil Underwood, who had long worked in the coal industry, received more than 20 percent of his campaign contributions and 30 percent of the cost of his million-dollar inauguration from coal.

AN OUTLAW INDUSTRY

Hechler predicted that as long as the coal industry dominated Appalachia, an inch of regulatory leeway would rapidly become miles of stripped land. From the beginning, West Virginia's regulations were peppered with omissions and innovative interpretations. Newly hired field inspectors were introduced to this "local version" of the law and in some cases did their work unaware that they were in violation of actual law. Patrick McGinley, a West Virginia University law professor and environmental litigator, recalls challenging illegally issued permits during the 1980s: "Virtually everything the law required was not being done. I had the agent who had issued the permits read the relevant section of SMCRA aloud to me. He said 'I've never seen that before.'"

Under a corrupt governor who would later land in federal prison, coal companies went on a binge in the 1980s, ignoring basic environmental standards and then ducking reclamation requirements by declaring bankruptcy and reconstituting themselves under different names. Investigative reporters, who did much of the enforcement agencies' job in this period, found multiple "companies" working in single underground mines and parent corporations spawning scores of short-lived offspring.

West Virginia's environmental regulators have shaped up considerably since then, but the DEP has kept the habit of collaborating with the coal industry, producing a tangled map of discrepancies between state practices and the language and intent of federal law. Most dramatically, SMCRA requires that after stripping, a company must restore the disturbed land to its "approximate original contour"—that is, put it back more or less the way it was. According to the original federal act, companies can be exempted from this requirement only when the leveled land is put to a new, productive, and valuable "commercial or recreational" use. The thrust of the law is that mountaintop removal might be an acceptable shortcut along the road to certain forms of economic development, but that otherwise mountains should be left as they are.

Yet most mountaintop jobs leave landscapes undeveloped and isolated. State agencies in Virginia and Kentucky permit mountaintop removal for "wildlife and forest management," a category broad enough to catch any swath of land where trees might someday grow or deer browse. West Virginia counts a company's promise to open exhausted mining sites to hunters and fishermen as sufficient to make the land a "recreational facility." But neither approach is more than a dodge since hardwood forests refuse to grow on strip-mined land: eliminating forests and streams does not improve wildlife habitat.

Even so, enforcement has been as lax as the state regulations are dubious. Ken Ward, Jr., a reporter with the Charleston Gazette, examined 81 permits for mountaintop removal operations and found that 61 did not include exemptions from the approximate original contour requirement. That is, 75 percent of the operations were illegal on their face. The DEP countered by arguing that since "contour" means shape, a change in altitude is irrelevant. That is to say, a company that drops a mountain 550 feet but leaves the bottom somewhat rugged has restored the site's approximate original contour. Removing a mountaintop, then, does not constitute mountaintop removal.

A suit now being prepared for the Highlands Conservancy, a West Virginia environmental group, requests that the state's regulation of mountaintop removal be brought back into sync with federal law. Beyond the approximate original contour question, the suit reminds the court that SMCRA requires a comprehensive study of how strip-mining affects water systems, which has not been conducted. The suit also asserts that the federal Clean Water Act bars the burial of steams with waste from mine sites. If upheld, this objection will mean that valley fills are simply illegal. Moreover, while SMCRA requires that a company post sufficient insurance or collateral to clean up the site should it go bankrupt or simply abscond, low-ball estimates and lax enforcement have left bond amounts well below the sums required to clean up abandoned sites. The OSM estimates the deficit at $60 million. Patrick McGinley puts it at ten times that amount.

LOOKING FOR THE FEDS

All of this takes place under the oversight of the Office of Surface Mining, the agency charged with ensuring that federal law is strictly enforced through a combination of field inspections and annual reviews of state programs. It's a demanding charge. SMCRA was an unusual piece of legislation. It contained elaborate requirements rather than broad guidelines for state programs, and mandatory citations and punishments for any violation. These stipulations were an acknowledgment that corrupt collaboration between government and industry was the rule in the coalfields, and that only strong national standards could end that pattern.

The program began auspiciously. President Jimmy Carter's OSM hired administrators and field inspectors who were known for their commitment to enforcement. Inspectors shut down illegal mines and brought irresponsible operators to heel, over sometimes violent resistance. A few inspectors were taken hostage by entire crews of angry miners.

Then, after Ronald Reagan's election in 1980, things began to fall apart. Interior Secretary James Watt appointed OSM administrators who had fought SMCRA in the courts. They promptly approved state programs that, according to an OSM official who was with the agency then, "did not in any way, shape, or form meet the federal standards." For much of the 1980s, the agency was strained by low-level warfare between would-be enforcers and Reagan appointees, with the latter slowly gaining ground. The program reached its nadir under George Bush's first OSM director, Harry Snider, who cut deals with companies to weaken enforcement, then imposed his arrangements in haranguing, late-night telephone calls to his underlings' homes. Bill Clinton's 1992 victory raised hopes among the remnants of the original OSM staff, who by then had become a corps of toughened dissidents. They have mostly been disappointed. President Clinton's first OSM director, Robert Uram, developed a reputation for indecisive leadership. Uram was widely perceived as caving in when the 1995 Republican Congress passed a 25 percent cut in the agency's program budget. The subsequent firings fell heavily on the corps of field inspectors, many of whom were precisely the same ones who had spent years resisting Reagan/Bush administrators.

Since then, OSM inspections of mining sites have fallen by as much as 50 percent in some states. People within the OSM describe the agency as isolated and nervous. Lacking active support from the Clinton administration, resented for its mere existence by industry, and scorned by disappointed environmentalists, the OSM is at constant risk of further cuts or complete elimination. From director Kathy Karpan to field inspectors, OSM agents tread carefully. Inspectors describe working to bury citizen complaints in communities where house foundations are cracked and water wells ruined by blasting. They know that the complaints are valid, but know also that they cannot uphold them without jeopardizing themselves or drawing fresh political attacks on the agency.

In recent months, citizen pressure and expressions of concern from two of West Virginia's congressional representatives have sparked the beginnings of federal action. The OSM has announced that West Virginia needs a clear definition of mountaintop removal. The Army Corps of Engineers has suggested that no new permits should be issued while the legal disputes surrounding the practice are settled. The EPA, which oversees the water-quality portions of strip-mining regulation, has warned against further relaxation of state law. However, permitting continues, and there has been no serious discussion of stopping ongoing mining.

Though the OSM now has almost no defenders, the agency remains the best hope for sound coal policy. Unless Democrats control both houses of Congress by a substantial margin, revisiting SMCRA could be disastrous. Although the OSM has permitted coal regulation to become a mockery of federal law, the agency remains better positioned than any other body to reinvigorate enforcement. Observers and OSM members agree that a few tactical appointments and a mandate from the secretary of the interior and the White House would be enough to revive the remaining inspectors and point the agency in the right direction. A push to restore the OSM's funding and rehire inspectors could also spur renewal. So far, the OSM remains a political orphan, and the land and people of the coalfields pay a stiff price for its abandonment.

COAL'S TRUE COST

The deterioration of mining regulation covers over a deeper set of questions. What are the longterm effects of removing mountaintops and filling valleys? Should mountaintop removal and other forms of strip-mining be legal? And should we rely as heavily as we do on coal?

No one knows what the legacy of mountaintop removal will be a century from now. Even the basic question of whether the valley fills will remain stable—a question inevitably posed in the shadow of the Buffalo Creek disaster—is uncertain: the West Virginia Division of Environmental Protection's Ed Griffith declares briskly, "I have complete confidence in the stability of those fills." In contrast, a former OSM employee who received a national award for his engineering work before leaving the agency says, "I'm very concerned. As time goes by, and these fills become saturated with water, they're going to begin to fail. I am convinced of that." There have been landslides reported at the feet of valley fills in Kentucky, but there is no consensus on whether those fills were representative or just exceptionally ill-engineered.

Another unanswered question is how stripping will affect Appalachia's waterways. River life depends on decaying leaves and other organic matter that small streams carry. But these delicate processes are diminished with every mile of valley fill. Moreover, no one knows how churning together complex layers of porous and nonporous rock will affect drainage patterns and water tables. Appalachia's water already carries a grim legacy of coal mining. Both strip-mining and traditional deep-mining disturb sulfur, which reacts with oxygen to produce acid water that can kill a creek. Roger Calhoun, director of the West Virginia OSM office, estimates that 2,000 miles of the state's rivers and streams are "severely impacted" by acid runoff and other mine pollutants, and that many of those waterways are dead. He also acknowledges that as hundreds of mines in the state's high-sulfur coalfields close and the operators cease treating nearby water, thousands more miles will be endangered.

All this means that while coal is the world's cheapest source of energy it is also the most laden with hidden costs—the dead lakes of Russia and corroded statues of Eastern Europe, for example, began with draglines and dynamite. Coal is the number one culprit in producing acid rain, causing 70 percent of the United States's sulfur dioxide emissions and much greater amounts in places that still depend heavily on high-sulfur coal. Burning coal produces twice as much carbon dioxide as natural gas and 50 percent more than oil and gasoline, making coal a leading cause of global warming. With the arguable exception of nuclear power, no other energy source displays such a dramatic gap between its immediate price tag and its true long-term costs.

These costs will not go down as long as mountaintop removal fits so readily into the logic of the country's energy economy. Berating the coal industry for destroying mountains and communities evades the reality that mining companies simply answer the country's everyexpanding appetite for cheap energy. West Virginia lawyer Tom Rodd, who won a landmark case in the early 1990s curbing some of the coal industry's worst excesses, judges that "West Virginia is the latest of the country's energy sacrifice zones, surrendered to keep power cheap. It isn't the first, and it may not be the last."

The best response to the disparity between coal's immediate and actual costs would be to change the terms of the fuel economy by erasing coal's artificial cheapness. Sound regulation and tax policy could build the environmental and social cost of mining and burning coal into its market price. Making coal more costly, in turn, would shift incentives throughout the economy, giving companies reason to invest in fuel-efficient technology and even nonpolluting energy sources. Simply enforcing SMCRA and the Clean Water Act also would have this effect, since responsible mining and restoration is more expensive than mountaintop removal. A bolder approach would revive the idea of a "carbon tax" on fossil fuel emissions, taxing energy use in proportion to the amount of greenhouse gas that it produces. By using carbon tax revenue to finance, say, a cut in the regressive and economically dampening payroll tax, lawmakers could re-orient the economy toward both high employment and clean technology.

The near demise of SMCRA also holds lessons for the conduct of public policy. One concerns the hazards of administrative law. Agencies like the OSM and DEP blend the functions of the executive, legislative, and judicial branches. They write regulations, sometimes departing significantly from the original intent of legislation, and establish interpretations of those regulations in their own administrative law courts. Administrative agencies have no direct, democratic accountability. Although citizen suits and political pressure sometimes affect agencies, regulatory law operates mainly beyond citizen's view. It is, however, subject to constant legal challenge and lobbying by industry's lawyers. Sometimes, as with SMCRA, it becomes nearly unrecognizable. Making administrative agencies more democratically accountable will hardly be a straightforward task, but it is an urgent one.

The fate of SMCRA also highlights the poverty of the current enthusiasm for state control of programs of every sort. The new federalism aims to let states work as laboratories for innovative policies and to permit state governments to respond to local conditions—social, economic, and ecological—that uniform national programs dough over. The history of mining regulation in West Virginia reminds us that those local conditions may include great disparities in political power, and sometimes even endemic corruption. Those problems occasioned the drive for federal standards in the first place, and they have not disappeared as federal policy has become less popular. Often, the challenge of effective government is not to unload federal programs but to make them work.

Although the coal industry is no longer the sole engine of Appalachia's economy, it has retained its political impunity. Musing on the days when he worked as a stripminer, Blair resident Carlos Gore observes wryly, "I reckon what goes around comes around." Asked if, by that principle, the coal bosses will get their comeuppance, he shakes his grizzled head: "The Lord don't seem to look on them that way." So far, the coal companies have been largely exempt from recompense and retribution even as their product has helped exempt the rest of the nation from environmental responsibility.

Any good resolution of the mountaintop removal struggle will have to break this vicious circle. And in so doing, it will necessarily address questions that run beyond strip-mining. Political commitment will have to overcome almost two decades of administrative neglect to revive the Office of Surface Mining. Political and ecological responsibility will have to take precedence over economic recklessness. Citizens will have to insist that market prices and profit margins should not alone determine the shape of the country's landscapes and communities. We will have to decide whether to maintain our comfort at the price of more sacrifice zones, with their dead towns and leveled mountains. In Appalachia, the time for a decision is running out.

CHAPTER 27

The Mountain Crafts: Romancing the Marketplace

by Garry Barker

Almost exactly 100 years ago, mountain "missionaries" were discovering the Appalachian treasure trove of crafts, that highly visible and marketable aspect of the culture which held appeal for the "outsiders" whose influence and money were needed to make things happen. Berea College President William G. Frost was making preparations for his horseback ride through Eastern Kentucky, West Virginia, East Tennessee, and Western North Carolina, a summer-long journey which would result in the formation of Berea's "Fireside Industries" crafts production and marketing program. In Madison County, North Carolina, Frances Louisa Goodrich was beginning the work which would create the living legend of Allanstand Cottage Industries.

The two unconnected efforts would later come together, join with forces from Penland, Brasstown, Gatlinburg, and the other more remote mountain pockets where settlement schools were preserving an almost artificial culture, and the lasting result was a regional phenomenon of craft training and marketing, promotion and publicity, and plenty of what David Whisnant would later term "cultural intervention."

So successful was this marketing of Appalachia's "culture" that Whisnant was to write, in 1983, "To this day there a thousand people who 'know' that mountaineers weave coverlets and sing ballads for every one who knows that millions of them have been industrial workers for a hundred years, have organized unions and picketed state and national capitols in pursuit of their constitutional rights. . . . Or that, today, they shop at K Mart and Radio Shack, drive Camaros, and watch as much television as people anywhere" (p. 33).

That conditioned, much-manipulated image of the quaint, crafts-making mountaineer has, for a century, been the cornerstone of a highly profitable Appalachian crafts marketing effort which continues today but now sells mostly the work of college trained designer-craftspeople.

Allen Eaton concluded his famed 1937 study *Handicrafts of the Southern Highlands* with these words: "To bring these people our civilization and yet save their culture is the task in which we should all have some part. There is but one approach to this task: that is the ethical approach which seeks, before imposing its own ideals on any person or

Source: From *Journal of the Appalachian Studies Association*, 5, 1993 by Garry Barker. Copyright © 1993 by Center for Appalachian Studies and Services. Reprinted by permission.

group, to draw from them the best they have to give" (p. 333).

To draw from them their best, then use that "best" as a marketing tool for products and a culture which bear but faint resemblance to the crafts and lifestyle of a century ago is truly our task, a jaundiced 1990s observer might conclude.

Perhaps the best example of the successful crafts marketing myth is the crooked-seamed brown Double Bowknot coverlet now owned by the Southern Highland Handicraft Guild and labeled, according to Jan Davidson in his introduction to the recently reprinted *Mountain Homespun,* as "the coverlet that started the Allanstand Industries."

> Before it was a museum piece, it [the coverlet] was used by Frances Goodrich to personify the continuity of her handcraft revival; to raise funds for craft programs, schools, and hospitals; to star in the most dramatic moment of Goodrich's *Mountain Homespun;* and to launch a business that ... survives to this writing.... Before Goodrich got it in 1895, it was a bedspread, probably greatly loved by an old mountain family because one of them made it completely herself. It is a crooked-seam coverlet made about 1850. (1990, p. 1)

The gift of the brown coverlet supposedly inspired Goodrich's work of reviving the weaving industry of Madison County, North Carolina, of building Allanstand into a craft business which became the foundation of the Southern Highland Handicraft Guild's sales success, and of the writing of *Mountain Homespun* and subsequent creation of the legend.

> "*Mountain Homespun's* central dramatic incident, the gift of the Double Bowknot, caught the attention of the feature writers, who retold it frequently and compared that gift to the gift of Allanstand [Miss Goodrich donated her business to the Guild in 1931] thus making the Guild the final step in conferring the management of mountain handcrafts from the family, to the saintly woman, to a corporation directed by northerners, to a coalition with other production centers." (Davidson 1990, p. 34)

Well before 1931, though, Berea College's subtle production and marketing influence had reached Goodrich, who brought Berea's Swedish looms to North Carolina and did away with the "crooked-seam" assembly method. The crooked seams were both practical (so the coverlet could be taken apart for cold water creek washing) and inevitable; early mountain looms were home-made, cumbersome affairs incapable of the precision weaving demanded by Goodrich and by the Northern marketplace. "The irony of the old brown Double Bowknot that started Allanstand—the grand icon of the Appalachian handcraft revival—is that it could not have been sold as an Allanstand coverlet, because, like most old mountain coverlets, it has crooked seams . . ." (Davidson 1990, p. 5). But the old Double Bowknot survives, and dramatic stage interpretations of Frances Goodrich's words from *Mountain Homespun* are used to perpetuate the myth which mothered a modern marketplace.

David Whisnant's scathing description of today's market must be considered:

> Cultural objects, styles, and practices introduced by intervenors sometimes prove remarkably durable, regardless of how little prior basis they had in the culture. The tens of thousands of tourists who visit the publicly funded Folk Art Center at the entrance to the Blue Ridge Parkway or troop through the craft shops of Gatlinburg or Asheville, and the millions who listen to folk-revival musicians on National Public Radio, are "seeing" and "hearing" continuity which is partial at best: they are buying the fruits of hybrid cultures that were long ago severely pruned and grafted. What they have in their shopping bags as they climb back into the station wagons and onto the tour buses is, to use a term familiar to cultural anthropologists, "airport culture." (1983, p. 262)

Whisnant does not deeply explore whether the native mountaineers were *willing* collaborators in the "cultural intervention" of the early twentieth century. I suspect they were, for financial gain.

Some economic truths heavily influenced the early work and established the pattern which still exists—the basic premise of crafts as an economic development tool. To succeed in the business world, crafts producers must make what the market will buy. "Bread and butter" production lines pay the bills for the craftspeople who depend upon sales for a livelihood. Early customers for coverlets from Berea College and Allanstand wanted handcrafted perfection, straight seams, and precise weaving, *done by the quaint and colorful mountaineers whom their purchases were helping to become more civilized.* The purchase was a multi-purpose transaction, then, part sentiment and missionary zeal, part insistence upon first-class quality and, as Allen Eaton once suggested, bargain prices (p. 287).

In regards to making what the market wants, little has changed. Like so many other native Appalachians who have learned to perform for pay—the Cherokees who pose in Comanche warbonnets for tourist dollars, the local musicians who learn to play the dulcimer and sing folksongs to have a chance at the contest cash prize, or Garry Barker slipping in and out of the East Kentucky dialect to earn his fee as after-dinner entertainment—the craftspeople have learned to give 'em what they want and laugh all the way to the bank.

The contemporary products most similar to the early coverlets are the quilts which now sell for $300 to $3,000 each, which seldom if ever are actually used on a working bed. The traditional everyday Appalachian quilt was a hodgepodge of fabric and color, made to be used, meant to keep people warm in unheated houses. There were, of course, "show-off" quilts, the "company quilts," fancy and tightly stitched artworks to impress the neighbors and the mother-in-law, and it is these special quilts which are the objects now of the collectors' lust. The modern marketplace quilts are made of new materials, in designer hues, as mass produced as the technique will permit, artful wall hangings meant for the interior designer trade. Machine-pieced quilts are becoming more commonplace and more accepted, and a spin-off industry of printed quilt patterns has evolved to fill the market demand.

It is the reality of the craft world to use technology and shortcuts to lessen the burden of production drudgery—to use electric potters' wheels, bandsaws and sanders, flyshuttle looms, gas-fired forges and pneumatic hammers, and even electric carving tools—but the concurrent reality is that customers must continue to believe the myth about quaint mountain craftspeople. Allen Eaton even subtly endorsed such an approach when he wrote:

> There is, however, no work so good but what some knowledge of the person who is doing it and the attendant circumstances will help make it more significant. . . . To appreciate it [the mountain craft] fully one must know something of the maker, his environment and his opportunities, or lack of opportunities. . . . The deep interest that many people feel in the Highlanders clusters about the true and quaint stories of them which have been captured by social workers, writers, and visitors to the region. To discard this element of appeal would be to throw away what is often a strong bond relating the possessor of an example of Highland handicraft to some mountain character, family, or group of neighbors. (1937, pp. 282–3)

We in the modern Appalachian craft world certainly have not discarded that "element of appeal," even though we have largely discarded the actual crafts and the "true and quaint" lifestyle of which Eaton wrote. Today in the newly-renovated Allanstand gallery in the Southern Highland Folk Art Center, you will find little or no "folk" art. You will find today's derivatives of the early crafts—nonfunctional baskets, art pottery, decorator quilts, brooms which cannot be used for sweeping, and cornshuck sculptures—plus the highly contemporary glass, wood, fiber, and clay works done by the skilled craftspeople who have moved to Appalachia to take advantage of the ready marketplace. You will also find the work of the hundreds of Appalachian craftspeople who carefully maintain and perpetuate the "quaint" image and prefer that the buying public never become aware that they (the quaint craftspeople) drive $18,000 vans, live in brick three-bedroom homes, watch cable television, and drink bottled water.

We all *are* willing participants in the marketing myth of quaint Appalachia, perfectly willing to swap image for cash-in-hand. Sometimes a perceptive observer can see the situation more clearly than can those of us whose daily lives are entwined with the marketplace, and Jim Wayne Miller perhaps described it best with his poem "The Brier Losing Touch With His Traditions":

> Once he was a chairmaker.
> People up north discovered him.
> They said he was "an authentic mountain craftsman."
> People came and made pictures of him working.
> wrote him up in the newspapers.
> He got famous.
> Got a lot of orders for his chairs.
> When he moved up to Cincinnati
> so he could be closer to his market
> (besides, a lot of his people lived there now)
> he found out he was a Brier.
>
> And when customers found out
> he was using an electric lathe and power drill
> just to keep up with all the orders,
> they said he was losing touch with his traditions.
> His orders fell off something awful.
> He figured it had been a bad mistake
> to let the magazine people take those pictures
> of him with his power tools, clean-shaven,
> wearing a flowered sports shirt and drip-dry pants.
>
> So he moved back down to east Kentucky.
> Had himself a brochure printed up
> with a picture of him using his hand lathe.
> Then when folks would come from the magazines,
> he'd get rid of them before suppertime
> so he could put on his shoes, his flowered sport shirt
> and double-knit pants, and open a can of beer
> and watch the six-thirty news on tv
> out of New York and Washington.
>
> He had to have some time to be himself. (1980, p. 44)

CHAPTER 25

From Farm to Coal Camp to Back Office and McDonald's: Living in the Midst of Appalachia's Latest Transformation

by Sally Ward Maggard

INTRODUCTION

As the principal fuel of industrialization throughout the twentieth century, coal is one of the world's most valued natural resources. The industrial development of the world's coal reserves involved social transformations of enormous scale. A substantial body of literature addresses these social changes, including research on the concentrated control and ownership of natural resources and land; the social transformation of pre-industrial economies and creation of coal communities; the creation of an industrial labor force; class divisions and conflict; regulation and management of the industry; workplace safety and health; the distribution of income, jobs and resources; and relationships between the state and capital in coal development.[1]

What is not well understood in the history and organization of coal mining is the importance of gender relations and gender ideology. This paper examines ways that gender shaped the mining of coal, the nature of local labor markets, and the structure and operation of households in the coalfields. Further, it argues that a particular mix of industrial heritage, culture, and gender shapes current economic restructuring in the coalfields, as well as policy initiatives promoted in the name of regional development.

APPALACHIAN COAL: A FACT OF INDUSTRIAL LIFE

One of the most important coal basins in the United States is in Central Appalachia, the source of more than half of the bituminous coal mined in the country and almost all U.S. coal exports (Harvey 1986). For over two hundred years miners have dug this coal from the ground, initially supplying fuel for blacksmiths and home heating, and then, as the nation industrialized, providing fuel for factories, steel mills, railroad boilers, and power plants (United Mine Workers of America 1976; Harvey 1986; Seltzer 1985). As early as 1914 the famous labor agitator, "Mother" Mary Harris Jones passionately extolled the importance of this labor:

"... in the last fifty years in the history of this nation look and see what the miners, and the miners alone, have done. Look at the thousands and hundreds of thousands of miles of railroads that you have built. Look at the liners that are

Source: From *Journal of the Appalachian Studies Association*, vol. 6, 1994 by Sally Ward Maggard. Copyright © 1994 by Center for Appalachian Studies and Services. Reprinted by permission.

plying the oceans, connecting nation with nation. Look at the telegraph lines, look at the streets, the subways, the elevated ways. Who has built them? The miners. You move the nation!" (quoted in Steel 1988, 143)

Since World War II, mechanization in mining has increased productivity but decreased the demand for human labor. This is illustrated by changes in mining employment in West Virginia, one of the most important Appalachian coal states. From 1950 to 1970 the state's mine work force fell by 70 percent, while productivity rose as the "continuous miner" replaced labor intensive pick and shovel mining methods. In 1967, the average coal miner produced 3,567 tons a year, up from a 1950 average of 1,217 tons (U.S. Bureau of Labor Statistics 1961). Over the next two decades an additional 30,000 mining jobs were lost (Nyden 1989) while productivity continued to climb with the introduction of long-wall technology. By 1988 the average West Virginia miner was producing 5,921 tons a year (Lewis 1992). These trends mean that while Appalachian coal remains viable in world coal trade, the industrial labor force and communities which have traditionally supported the development and growth of the industry are in crisis. To understand the crisis and the nature of its impact, it is important to review industrial history and consider the structure of local coal economies as the region entered its current era of transformation.

GENDER AND INDUSTRIAL HISTORY IN COAL MINING

In the initial phases of coal development, an industrial infrastructure was carved from rural, independent agricultural economies in Central Appalachia (Billings, Blee, Swanson 1986). This involved purchasing and clearing timber, buying coal rights and land, brokering financial packages between investors and producers, extending rail transport into coal regions, constructing the industrial sites themselves, constructing coal camps and towns, and recruiting an industrial labor force (Lewis 1992; Eller 1982; Maggard 1981).

In general, women were not in positions to direct this industrial development. Most of the necessary productive assets were and continue to be owned and managed by men: land, capital, geological survey capability, technology, and labor. Decisions to sell agricultural land and/or rights to minerals underneath the land were usually made by male members of households (Weise 1993). Similarly, decisions to relocate families to the new coal camps were usually made by men (Coles and Coles 1978; Kahn 1972; see also González 1991; Flynt 1986). Women were largely on the sidelines as ownership and control over natural resources were negotiated, and again as the necessary infrastructure was constructed. Corporate decisions about the composition of the labor force, efficient ways to support and reproduce that labor force, and tolerable degrees of economic diversity resulted in a rigid division and valuing of labor by sex in the coalfields. Production jobs in the mines were reserved for men, recruited to constitute a "judicious mix" of mountain farmers, foreign immigrants, and southern blacks (Lewis 1987; Bailey 1973). Women were assigned to the "auxiliary" work of managing households and caring for dependents and the disabled.

A family settlement pattern in the coal camps served to "discipline" miners, provide unpaid domestic service to support the mine labor force, and increase profits for owners and stockholders. The thousands of men recruited to mine coal were housed near mine sites with the family members who fed them, cleaned their clothes, and cared for them when injured or sick. Miners' wages were recycled in company owned stores and rents. The presence of wives and children acted as a stabilizing force, discouraging absenteeism and high employee turnover (Pudup 1990; Simon and Justice 1981; U.S. Department of Labor 1925).[2]

For men, leaving agriculture for coal mining meant working inside the coal mines in exchanges for wages. Men lost control over the means of economic production, but their labor was understood as central to the economy. Women, too, lost control over the means of production. Now their economic survival depended on their connections to the men in their households who earned miners' wages.[3]

Women had been directly involved in all phases of rural production in farm economies (Pudup 1990; Verhoeff 1917). In the coal camps, women found that many of their agricultural skills were necessary for survival. Gardening and livestock raising were widespread, and small-scale home production of goods stretched miners' wages (Pudup 1990; Trotter 1990; Lewis 1989). In addition, some women in mining camps earned income by taking in boarders and doing laundry.

Although almost all women worked without pay inside their households, some women found employment in and around the Central Appalachian coal camps (Pudup 1990). Mining increased the need for rural hospitals, and some women learned nursing through a system of apprenticeships (Maggard 1988). As domestic servants and seamstresses, some women provided goods and services for middle and upper income residents of coal towns. Others worked as teachers in company towns.

Overall, there were few opportunities for waged work in mining regions for women or for men. Economic activity centered on a single industry. Competition among many coal producers and from other fuels intensified pressures to keep production costs low, resulting in severe measures to control the work force (Dix 1988; Seltzer 1985). Owners opposed a diversified local economy that could create competition for labor and could inflate wages above levels set by the industry. As a result, most men worked in mining, some in forestry and agriculture. Others worked in construction, building coal camps, mines, rail lines, and new buildings in the expanding county seat towns (Maggard 1981). Most women did the less visible, unpaid work required in social reproduction and household management.[4]

A two-pronged, gendered ideology emerged to justify this division and unequal valuing of labor. The ideology of the "male breadwinner" first of all assigned women's "proper" place to domestic labor inside coal camps.[5] Second, it assigned men's "proper" place to the dangerous work of mining coal. Ideas of femininity and masculinity came to be tied up with this allocation of labor and reinforced economic arrangements, as the issue of coal mine safety and health illustrates.

The coal industry in the United States has a dismal health and safety record (Curran 1993; National Research Council 1982; McAteer 1973), and mining is consistently ranked as the most or second most dangerous industry in the country. Industry representatives have been quick to argue that little can be done to change this, that fate, nature, and carelessness of miners themselves are to be blamed for the death, injury, and disease that plagues coal mining. Comparative research on mine safety and health, however, demonstrates tremendous variation among industrialized nations and challenges such explanations (McAteer and Galloway 1980; Drury 1965). The position that mining is "naturally" dangerous excuses unsafe working conditions and mining practices and appalling rates of injury and death. Reserving mining jobs for men and then equating masculinity with the daily risk of death and disability makes men the principle victims. Both notions work to keep production costs low in mining.

The belief that coal mining should be reserved for men has kept women out of mining jobs throughout most of the history of the industry. In the United States women were able to break through this cultural barrier and force their way into these industrial jobs only in the 1970s (Hall 1980; Scott 1977).[6] "Women's work" has always involved heavy physical labor and long hours. Furthermore, women have suffered terrible rates of injury and death in other industrial labor (Groneman and Norton 1987; Milkman 1985; Conway 1979). In an economy dominated by a single industry, the argument that women should not work in that industry because it is dangerous reserved the highest paid employment in the local economy for men.

In the Appalachian coalfields, cultural norms segregating "men's work" and "women's work" and identifying males as the sole providers of the "family wage" functioned as powerful ideological supports for the economic system that developed in coal. They defined men as expendable, left women dependent on these men, and assigned women to perform unpaid domestic labor. The situation left working class women and men extremely vulnerable.

This mix of industrial history and culture structured occupational opportunity and the quality of work life throughout much of this century. Men's work has been higher waged and more highly valued, but dependent on changing technologies in the production process and on fluctuating demand in the world coal market. Women's work has consistently been understood as secondary to men's work, as supplementing income earned by a male "breadwinner." Much of women's work has been highly productive and located within households, but it remained unwaged and, in effect, invisible.

From the earliest period of industrialization in coal, then, local economies were sharply segregated by sex in terms of work and income. This segregation was overlain with and supported by gendered ideology. Patterns of economic opportunity, earning capacity, market and household divisions of labor, and gendered self-identities which characterize the coalfields today can be traced to this period of industrial history.

LOCAL LABOR MARKETS, GENDER, AND RESTRUCTURING

One indication of the legacy of this economic history is the pattern of men's and women's participation in the formal labor force. Table 1 compares labor force participation rates in the United States with West Virginia for selected periods from 1900 to 1990. Two patterns are evident. First, both men's and women's labor participation has been consistently lower in West Virginia than the national average. Second, women's participation rates in West Virginia have been dramatically lower than men's, the lowest of any state in the nation throughout most of this century. These patterns are related to the structure of occupational opportunity and to the rigidly sex segregated

Table 1 Civilian Labor Force Participation Rates* for United States and West Virginia by Sex, 1900–1990

	Male		Female	
	United States	*West Virginia*	*United States*	*West Virginia*
1900	88.0%	80.0%	18.0%	90.0%
1930	84.1%	72.4%	21.9%	13.1%
1950	78.9%	74.6%	27.8%	19.6%
1960	83.3%	67.8%	37.7%	24.3%
1970	79.7%	66.0%	43.3%	29.4%
1980	77.4%	68.4%	51.5%	36.5%
1990	76.1%	64.6%	57.5%	42.6%

*Rates are calculated for persons gainfully employed according to age thresholds which change over time. The Census counted persons 10 years of age and above through 1930; persons 14 and above in 1940 and 1950; persons 16 and above since 1960.
Source: U.S. Census of Population, U.S. Bureau of Labor Statistics, and Statistical Abstract of the U.S. for selected years.

roles that have characterized West Virginia's economy.[7]

A second legacy of West Virginia's economic history is the pattern of employment across industrial sectors. As late as 1970, the economy of Central Appalachia was less diversified than the nation as a whole in terms of population employed in different industries (Appalachian Regional Commission 1979). Fewer people in the region worked in retail and wholesale trade, professional services, manufacturing, domestic and entertainment services, finance, insurance and real estate, business and repair services and construction than in the nation as a whole. Far more people, however, worked in mining, forestry, and educational services.

Table 2 illustrates the lack of industrial diversification in West Virginia in 1980 and 1990, and its relationship to the sex segregation of the labor force. In 1980 and 1990, men's employment was concentrated in four industrial sectors: mining, manufacturing, construction, and retail trade. Women's employment was concentrated in three sectors: retail trade, health services, and education, but with some concentration in manufacturing.

Within those industrial sectors in which women work, their jobs are often clustered at the low-waged end of an industry. For instance, in 1990 of all people employed in manufacturing in West Virginia, men (83.4 percent) were far more likely than women (16.6 percent) to be producing chemicals and allied products. Women (87.1 percent) were far more likely than men (12.9 percent) to be working in apparel and other finished textile products. The average wage in chemical manufacturing in 1990 was $804.13 a week. In contrast, the average weekly wage in apparel and textile manufacturing was $191.01 a week (WVBEIS 1991). Overall, this means that women are at a disadvantage relative to men in terms of earning power. In 1990 employed women earned only fifty cents for every dollar men earned. West Virginia men with high school degrees had incomes greater than women with seven years or more of college (U.S. Bureau of Census 1990; West Virginia Women's Commission 1993).

Taken together, these data describe an undiversified and sex-segregated economy with particularly severe consequences for women. Women's participation in the labor force has been low, the range of opportunity for participation has been narrow, and the wages women have earned have been low. While men have traditionally had more options and worked in higher waged jobs than women, they, too have been constrained by a limited range of job choices. These patterns trace back to the industrial order created with industrialization in coal. Today, these patterns are dramatically changing, and women and men are experiencing the changes in very different ways.

During the 1980s, the economy in West Virginia moved from its traditional base in extractive and manufacturing industries toward an economy based in the production of services (Table 3). In 1979, mining was the largest industry in West Virginia in terms of earnings. By 1989, the largest industries in the state in terms of earnings were in services, accounting for 21.2 percent of all earnings. These developments represent an important shift in the structure of the economy in just one decade.

From 1977 to 1987, the state lost almost 70,000 mining and manufacturing jobs. In mining, 27,332 jobs were lost at the same time that coal production rose. Over this period, mining jobs averaged $36,400 in annual wages. Manufacturing, averaging $20,000 a year, declined by 41,823 jobs, primarily in metal and chemical industries. Other high waged sectors that decreased dramatically include construction (down by 13,056 jobs, average wages $20,000 a year) and transportation and utilities (down by 16,030 jobs, average wages $30,000 a year). Employment in mining has continued to plummet, dropping by 21.7 percent from 1985 to 1990 (Center for Economic Research 1991a).

Overall, during the past decade the economy created relatively few new jobs in West Virginia and these were concentrated in lower waged industrial sectors, especially in services.[8]

Table 2 Industry of Employed Persons for West Virginia by Sex: 1980–1990

Denominators = Total Employed Persons 16 Years and Over in 1980 (689,461) and 1990 (671,085)

Industry	1980 Number	%	1990 Number	%	% Change	Males 1980 Number	%	Males 1990 Number	%	Females 1990 Number	%	% Change
Total Employed Persons	430,240	100.0	381,984	100.0		259,221	100.0		100.0	289,101	100.0	0.0
Agriculture, forestry, fishing	8,924	1.3	10,197	1.5	+0.2	2,311	0.3		0.3	2,307	0.3	0.0
Mining (coal, oil, gas)	65,983	9.6	34,488	5.1	−4.5	3,265	0.5		0.3	1,924	0.3	−0.2
Construction	48,437	7.0	43,262	6.4	−0.6	3,742	0.5		0.5	3,593	0.5	0.0
Manufacturing	8,139	14.2	75,462	11.2	−3.0	28,443	4.1		3.5	24,279	3.5	−0.6
–Apparel, textiles	709	0.1	586	0.1	0.0	4,586	0.7		0.6	3,961	0.6	−0.1
–Printing, publishing	3,494	0.5	3,970	0.6	+0.1	2,353	0.3		0.4	2,969	0.4	+0.1
–Chemicals and allied products	23,304	3.4	15,377	2.3	−1.1	3,471	0.5		0.4	3,066	0.4	−0.1
Transportation	26,118	3.8	24,182	3.6	−0.2	4,575	0.7		0.8	5,583	0.8	+0.1
Communication and other public utilities	18,555	2.7	17,434	2.6	−0.1	6,785	1.0		0.9	6,139	0.9	−0.1
Wholesale trade	19,207	2.8	17,399	2.6	−0.2	5,158	0.7		0.7	5,142	0.7	0.0
Retail trade	51,783	7.5	56,083	8.4	+0.9	56,917	8.3		9.7	66,739	9.7	+1.4
–General merchandise stores	3,869	0.6	3,913	0.6	0.0	11,164	1.6		1.6	10,806	1.6	0.0
–Food, bakery, dairy stores	11,015	1.6	11,515	1.7	+0.1	9,888	1.4		1.9	12,824	1.9	+0.5
–Eating, drinking places	7,522	1.1	11,386	1.7	+0.6	15,989	2.3		3.0	20,403	3.0	+0.7
–Auto dealers, auto supply	9,364	1.4	6,972	1.0	−0.4	1,865	0.3		0.2	1,525	0.2	−0.1
Finance, business related services	22,042	3.2	26,974	4.0	+0.8	19,232	2.8		3.9	25,830	3.9	+1.1
Personal services, including household	5,510	0.8	5,963	1.6	+0.8	15,214	2.2		2.1	14,722	2.1	−0.1
Entertainment, recreation services	2,889	0.4	4,308	0.6	+0.2	2,216	0.3		0.4	2,982	0.4	+0.1
Health services, including hospitals	12,132	1.8	13,876	2.1	+0.3	41,533	6.0		7.7	52,871	7.7	+1.7
Other professional, related services	9,843	1.4	13,523	2.0	+0.6	10,006	1.5		3.0	19,844	3.0	+1.5
Education	22,862	3.3	23,080	3.4	+0.1	42,306	6.1		6.3	43,213	6.3	+0.2
Public administration	17,816	2.3	15,753	2.4	+0.1	17,518	2.5		2.0	13,933	2.0	−0.5

Source: Detailed Population Characteristics. Part 50. West Virginia. 1980 Census of Population. November 1983. STF4 1990 Census of the Population. June 1993.

Table 3 Largest Industries and Percent of Earnings of Employed Persons for West Virginia: 1989 and 1979

Industry	Percent Earnings
1989	
Services	21.2
State, local government	13.3
Manufacturing, durable goods	10.8
Mining	10.5
1979	
Mining	14.9
Manufacturing	14.6
Services	12.7
State, local government	11.0

Source: Center for Economic Research (1991a).

Between 1977 and 1987 there were 31,988 new service sector jobs, but they averaged only $15,000 a year in wages. The dominant service industry in West Virginia is now health services, but 62 percent of that employment is in the lower waged non-profit sector (Center for Economic Research 1991b). Other new jobs (over 9,000) were created in retail trade, but they averaged only $13,000 a year in wages. The 4,784 new jobs in finance, insurance, and real estate during this period averaged $14,500 a year in wages (Center for Economic Research 1991a).

The consequences of this economic restructuring for West Virginia are staggering. Many people have simply left the state. The population declined by 8 percent from 1980 to 1990. Forty four of the state's fifty five counties lost population over the decade (U.S. Bureau of Census 1990). After the 1990 Census, West Virginia lost one of its four U.S. House of Representative seats.

Earnings fell substantially. West Virginia ranked 50th in the nation in per capita income in 1989, dropping down from 47th in 1979. In the same period, median household income fell 14.8 percent (adjusting for inflation in consumer prices). The poverty rate for families rose from 11.7 percent in 1979 to 16 percent in 1989, and almost one quarter of the population now lives in poverty (Center for Economic Research 1991a).

Since the mid-1970s, the unemployment rate in West Virginia has been higher than the average national rate, and in 1992 it reached 11.4 percent. In coal counties like McDowell, Wyoming, Boone, Logan, and Marion, unemployment that year ranged from 13 to 22.7 percent higher than the state average (Yoder 1993). Two thirds of the 64,000 West Virginians who were out of work in 1990 had "fresh" work experience. That is, 66.5 percent of West Virginia's unemployed people in 1990 had just lost their jobs and were looking for work (Pitcher 1992).

Restructuring is felt in different ways by women and by men. Female-headed households are particularly vulnerable and represent the fastest growing group among the poverty population. A stunning 55 percent of West Virginia families with a female head and related children under the age of eighteen (no husband present) were below poverty level in 1989. The comparable figure in 1979 was 43.4 percent (U.S. Bureau of Census 1990, 1983).

The changing economic structure creates new opportunities and new disadvantages for women and men to earn income. Most of the industrial sectors that are shrinking are those which have traditionally employed men. Most of those that are growing have traditionally employed women (Table 4). This mismatch between new jobs and the skills of the unemployed means that unemployed coal miners and manufacturing workers are unlikely to fill new jobs in services and retail trade. Differences in male and female labor force participation rates from 1980 to 1990 reflect this problem. The female rate increased by 6.1 percent, while the male rate fell by 3.8 percent.[9] As a result, state economic forecasts do not project a drop in unemployment with current job creation (Center for Economic Research 1993).

Growth and decline trends of the late 1980s are expected to continue in West Virginia. Occupation projections to the year 2000 show most job openings in retail and services and the fewest in manufacturing related occupations (Culp et.al. 1991). Since new jobs in services and retail employment are in low-waged industries, these changes promise to impoverish households. Further, they may translate into realignments of gender relations inside families. Males, the predominant household "breadwinners" in the coalfields since early in the century, are losing their positions in the region's economy. Women, on the other hand, are moving into the paid labor force in ever larger numbers, even if they still participate at lower than national rates.

There is evidence that restructuring creates tremendous strains inside households. Layoffs in coal mines tend to be followed by spikes in the incidence of domestic violence. The Women's Shelter in Charleston, West Virginia, was able to map a pattern during 1980–1982, a period of severe mine layoffs. Within two days of each announced layoff the number of calls received on domestic violence doubled (Ewen 1989).

Against the current economic insecurity, even jobs that pay only $4.50 an hour look good to many West Virginians. Chronically high and worsening unemployment, high underemployment (when skills far outstrip demands of current jobs), and a large reserve of women poised to enter the labor force mean West Virginia has a plentiful—and needy—supply of labor. As the state's industrial structure shifts and service industries and retail trade expand, employers expecting to fill jobs with low paid (but highly productive) workers find West Virginia attractive.

Table 4 Performance of West Virginia Industry: Percentage Change in Employment 1985–1990

Industry	% Change
Top Ten Performers	
Social Services	50.0
Special Trade Contractors	25.3
Lumber, Wood Products	24.2
Health Services	24.1
Eating and Drinking Places	22.9
Apparel and Accessory Stores	20.8
Amusement Services	20.4
Hotels, Other Lodging	16.4
Miscellaneous Retail	16.3
Food Stores	14.8
Bottom Ten Performers	
Apparel and Other Textile Products	–4.4
Food and Kindred Products	–6.7
General Merchandise Stores	–11.4
Chemicals and Allied Products	–11.5
Fabricated Metal Products	–13.9
Electronic, Electrical Equipment	–16.1
Oil and Gas Extraction	–19.3
Stone, Clay and Glass Products	–21.2
Coal Mining	–21.7
Textile Mill Products	–76.9

Source: West Virginia Bureau of Employment Programs; prepared by Center for Economic Research (Culp et.al. 1991).

ECONOMIC REVITALIZATION AND REINDUSTRIALIZATION

Local and state development officials have outlined several economic revitalization priorities for West Virginia. Two that have been successful in creating new jobs include a program to attract "back offices" to the state, and efforts to expand tourism. Both represent economic growth strategies that rest on a low-waged, heavily female labor force.

Back offices are decentralized production sites housing operations of service and manufacturing companies. Employees may work at data entry and processing, market research, telemarketing, medical transcription, publishing, customer service, financial services, and piece-rate assembly. Companies dividing up and reorganizing labor into dispersed operations look for a dependable, hard working but inexpensive labor force, along with cheap office space and a business climate which supports the externalization of production costs. Wages tend to be low, and work is often part-time (Dickstein 1992).

To tempt these and other companies to relocate operations to West Virginia, the state government offers an array of financial incentives including tax credits, pre-hiring screening, training subsidies, and loan programs (Fladung 1992). West Virginia's Super Tax Credit, for example, allows recovery of up to 90 percent of capital investment through state tax credits.

A joint project with Bell Atlantic and state government called "Office of the Future" markets the state to the information services industry, while simultaneously promoting West Virginia's state of the art fiber optic and digital telecommunications system.[10] Bell Atlantic researched the suitability of West Virginia as a location site for such back offices and concluded that one of the state's most important assets is its labor force (Pitcher 1992).

Comments from executives interviewed for the study expose the painful twists economic restructuring has created for workers. Executives of five companies now operating in the state talked about the ease with which they staff their offices. Chilton Research, for instance, closed two Pennsylvania offices and moved to Charleston. According to Andy Lohan of Chilton, ". . . in Charleston we can fill them [jobs] and fill them when we need to fill them. Labor is so much more available in Charleston" (Pitcher 1992, p. 7). By word of mouth and few, if any, advertisements, Chilton keeps its part-time work force of between 50 and 250 employees at capacity, paying $4.25 a hour to start. Other companies report word-of-mouth hiring. Roberta Fowlkes of Bell Atlantic commented, "We've never had to advertise, and there were just hundreds of applicants just from the announcement. . . . We have no problem getting the people" (Pitcher 1992, p. 8).

Who are these people flocking to low paid, often part-time, back office jobs? According to Bell Atlantic's research, three groups of people make up a pool of workers ripe for these jobs. First, an estimated 350,000 underemployed people in West Virginia represent "an experienced, enthusiastic pool of potential office workers" ready to work for low hourly wages (Pitcher 1992, p. 7). Second, a large pool of "voluntary nonparticipants" exists in West Virginia's "hidden" labor force. These are people the federal government defines as "discouraged workers," out of work so long that they have given up looking for new jobs. According to Bell Atlantic, such "experienced people will quickly put themselves back into the job market when they see that there are jobs available" (Pitcher 1992, p. 12).

Women constitute the third group in the hidden labor pool Bell Atlantic discovered in West Virginia. According to the study, the very presence of service sector employment acts as "a driver of higher female participation" (Pitcher 1992, p. 12). Of course, the very absence of other alternatives may be a more likely "driver" of women who move into the new back office jobs. The dramatic decline in mining, manufacturing, and construction jobs, the decline in per capita and household income, and the lack of other employment options combine to make such service jobs attractive to women, not just the lure of keypunching and data entry in a job processing medical insurance claims.

Tourism is a second industrial sector that experienced job growth in the 1980s in West Virginia. Three of the top ten job growth industries in the state—eating and drinking places, amusement services, and hotels and other lodging—are clearly related to growth in tourism, as is growth in miscellaneous retail trade and food stores (Table 4). Women are heavily represented in the labor force of all of these expanding industries, earning low wages and few, if any, benefits and often working on a seasonal and part-time basis. For example, women's employment in eating and drinking places grew over the decade, but wages in 1990 averaged only $130.61 per week, making this one of the lowest paid sectors in retail trade (WVBEIS 1991).

Michal Smith has produced a blistering critique of promoting tourism as an economic development savior. By analyzing an array of social and economic indicators, Smith found that the quality of life did not improve in eighty-four rural counties in twelve southeastern states where the tourist industry grew from 1970 to 1984. Tourist dependent counties had higher unemployment and higher rates of poverty than counties with a more diverse economic base. "Prosperity," Smith concluded, "simply failed to 'trickle down'" from this boom in tourist industry development (1989, v).

Smith's research demonstrates that the impact of development strategies is felt unevenly in an economy. In particular, Smith found that patterns of economic benefit and loss associated with tourism expansion follow sex and race divisions in local economies. Poverty rates, for instance, were especially high in households headed by women.

Tourism, it turns out, provides jobs for women, but these jobs are marginal, seasonal, low-waged jobs in food service, retail sales, and hotel service. Construction work generated by tourism expansion is dominated by males, as is the small pool of managerial jobs which results. African Americans fare so terribly in the tourist industry that, according to Smith, they leave the region. This research indicates that growth in tourism, like the growth of "back office" employment, may offer the good news of "new jobs," but does not guarantee a recovering state economy or renewed economic security for West Virginia households and communities.

CONCLUSIONS

For well over a century, business investment and industrial development in Appalachia has been closely aligned with a system of gender relations and gender ideology. Mixing cultural norms and beliefs about men's work and women's work made good business sense in coal mining. The production costs of labor and work site preparation were kept low by equating masculinity with a willingness to work in dangerous conditions and by defining men as expendable, easy to replace after injury and death or through investment in highly productive new technologies.

Other production costs—those associated with the social reproduction of the labor force and management of households—were written off and devalued by defining them as "proper" nonwaged, work for women. Women in paid labor earned low wages since their work was considered auxiliary to the family wage that men earned at the mines.

The economic system that took form around industrial development in coal is now being pulled apart. The cultural ideal of a male breadwinner who is sole supporter of spouse and dependent children is not achievable in the emerging economy. Women are moving into paid labor, even if much of it is low waged, and men are being displaced from those jobs that drove a single-industry and sex-segregated economy. This promises a social transformation as profound as the one that carved out the coalfields at the beginning of this century.

New strategies to make profits in the region seize on the patterns in this economic change. A desperate, skilled, willing to work, and inexpensive labor force promises a supply of cheap labor. State governments struggling to "create jobs" provide investment incentives to companies eager to find cheap labor. These new investment patterns do not necessarily promise widespread well being or economic health in the region.

Scholars and government planners alike need to raise careful questions about the development strategies they study or embrace. Some policies have the effect of carving up the labor force into especially vulnerable sections and treating these vulnerabilities as state or regional "assets." Because of the economic history of the coalfields and its integral gender differences, different outcomes of development initiatives for women and men are expected.

The Appalachian coalfield region is witnessing the disassembling of a nearly century old economic and domestic arrangement. Development that merely exploits these changes for profit is not likely to move the Appalachians coalfields out of crisis. Instead, it is likely to leave residents of the region mired in the very persistent poverty that has been its mark throughout much of this century.

CHAPTER 33

The Grass Roots Speak Back

by Stephen L. Fisher

Contrary to popular images of Appalachians as passive victims, there exists throughout the Appalachian Mountains a tradition of individual and organized citizen efforts to establish community services and preserve community values. This essay describes the variety and extent of local and regional efforts for change in Appalachia since 1960 and examines the lessons to be learned from these efforts.[1]

The Appalachian region has never lacked a politics of change and alternative development. But what stands out in the literature describing life in Appalachia before 1960 is not the extent of change efforts but rather the obstacles to change, the conditions leading to quiescence.[2] The industrialization of Appalachia was characterized by single-industry economies, the control of land and resources by large absentee companies, high levels of poverty and unemployment, the frequent use of red baiting, intimidation, and physical force to squelch dissent, political corruption, and a highly stratified and oppressive class system. Collective struggles for change were further undermined by cultural traditions that stressed individualism, by the strength of capitalist ideology, by racism and sexism, by the lack of strong local organizations, by high illiteracy rates, and by poor transportation and communication systems.

During this period, one could find throughout Appalachia examples of the starkest political and economic oppression in American society. In recent years, anthropologists and social and feminist historians have taught us that, when faced with such repressive conditions, people find ways to resist. This was certainly true in Appalachia. The organized efforts of workers in the coal, textile, and steel industries to improve their working and living conditions are well documented. But in other parts of the Appalachian Mountains, responses to these conditions often assumed forms far less visible than picket lines and organized movements and included such individual acts of behavior as gossip, back talk, holding on to one's dialect, refusal to cooperate with outside authority figures, and migration. This type of protest is part of what James Scott refers to as the "hidden transcript" of the oppressed.[3]

Increasingly, Appalachian scholars are coming to recognize the existence and importance of such protest in Appalachia's history and to understand that it has most frequently occurred

Source: From *Confronting Appalachian Stereotypes: Back Talk from an American Region* by Billings, Norman & Ledford, ed. Copyright © 1999 by University Press of Kentucky. Reprinted by permission.

in struggles to preserve traditional values and ways of life against the forces of modernization. For example, Helen Lewis, Sue Kobak, and Linda Johnson describe the various ways in which mountain families and churches became defensive and inward in order to protect their members from some of the harmful impacts of industrialization and the actions of outside change agents.[4] Kathleen Blee and Dwight Billings reinterpret early ethnographic studies of the region to show that work attitudes and other practices previously viewed as traits of a culture of poverty could better be understood as forms of resistance to the capitalist separation of work and control.[5] Altina Waller argues that the legendary Hatfield-McCoy feud can be seen as a battle between local defenders of community autonomy and outside industrial interests.[6] These and similar studies broaden our understandings of the nature and extent of resistance by rural working-class and poor people in Appalachia 1960.

Many of the obstacles that made collective struggles so difficult throughout Appalachia's history are still present today, and individual protests continue on a number of fronts. But new conditions after 1960 provided impetus and support to organized resistance efforts throughout Appalachia. The civil rights movement helped legitimize the notion of dissent in general and the strategy of nonviolent civil disobedience in particular throughout the region and the nation. The environmental and women's movements offered models and resources for local groups in the mountains. Moreover, these movements provided the impetus for national legislation that created opportunities for local organizations fighting to save their land and communities from environmental destruction or working to create alternative economic opportunities for women. The antiwar and student movements called into question the notions of progress, modernization, and national interest that had been used for so long to justify the destruction of traditional ways of life in Appalachia.

The War on Poverty spawned the Appalachian Volunteers and community action agencies throughout the mountains. While these programs had many weaknesses, they did bring young organizers into the region and provided opportunities for local leadership development. Mainstream churches, reflecting a new social consciousness, sent to Appalachia clergy and other church workers who were committed to working for social and economic justice. The construction of more and better roads, the availability of video recording equipment, open meeting and record laws, and increased church and foundation funding of Appalachian citizen groups also contributed to local organizing efforts.

These and other factors led to an outburst of grassroots community organizing across Appalachia in the late 1960s and early 1970s. Local residents fought to prevent the destruction of their land and homes by strip miners, dam and highway builders, the U.S. Forest Service, toxic waste dumpers, and recreation and second-home developers. People organized to secure welfare benefits, to enact tax reform, to build rural community centers and health clinics, to fight for better schools for their children, and to establish programs in literacy and child care. Community groups pursued a wide variety of alternative economic development strategies that resulted in agricultural and craft cooperatives, worker-owned factories, and new job opportunities for women. Efforts to preserve and celebrate local culture flourished in the mountains, as people began to develop a consciousness of and pride in being Appalachian.

In the 1990s people across Appalachia are still fighting back, often around similar issues.[7] The battle over strip mining continues as local groups challenge the Office of Surface Mining's nonenforcement of the federal strip mining law and join with other groups to lobby Washington for better water protection laws. Communities throughout rural Appalachia struggle to prevent their landfills from becoming the dumping grounds for the nation's trash, sludge, and toxic waste. The Yellow Creek Concerned Citizens and the Dayhoit Concerned Citizens in east Kentucky, the Dead Pigeon River Council and the Oak Ridge Environmental Peace Alliance in East Tennessee, and the Dickenson County Citizens Committee in Southwest Virginia are just a few of the groups across the region fighting the poisoning of their land, air, and water. The Ohio Valley Environmental Coalition organizes around industrial pollution where Ohio, Kentucky, and West Virginia meet. The Ivanhoe Civic League and the Dungannon Development Commission in Southwest Virginia and the Appalachian Center for Economic Networks in Athens, Ohio, pursue innovative grassroots alternative economic development plans. The Mountain Women's Exchange in East Tennessee and Women and Employment in West Virginia work to improve the economic position of women in the region.

In sum, since the 1960s, hundreds of new citizen groups have been organized throughout Appalachia. Most arose in response to a particular issue. These single-issue groups have worked together from time to time, helped create local leadership, and won important victories. But because they have focused on a single issue, many of these groups have been short-lived, disappearing once their issue has been resolved. Thus, one of the most exciting and hopeful developments in community organizing in Appalachia in recent years has been the establishment and success of thriving and influential multi-issue, membership-driven organizations such as Save Our Cumberland Mountains (SOCM), Kentuckians for the Commonwealth (KFTC), and the Community Farm Alliance (CFA).

SOCM, organized in 1972 to fight strip mining in a five-county area in the northern coalfields of Tennessee, changed from a single-issue, staff-run group to a multi-issue, grassroots organization able to exercise power and influence at the state and national levels.[8] KFTC, started in mid-1981 by a small group of eastern Kentucky residents who wanted to address community problems that crossed county lines, has grown into a statewide, multi-issue, social justice organization of more than twenty-three hundred members in ninety counties.[9] CFA was transformed from a handful of people who were replicating the mistakes of the national farm movement of the 1980s to a growing and successful membership-based organization with over a dozen chapters across Kentucky.[10]

These organizations stress the significance of local indigenous leadership recruitment and training, shared and long-term consciousness raising, the development of internal democratic social relations, ideological patience, and the willingness to connect with people as they are. Their success illustrates the importance of using county chapters to build statewide organizations and of connecting local issues to state, national, and global patterns and concerns.

Since the 1960s, activists have attempted to organize citizen organizations in the Appalachian Mountains into a regionwide grassroots social movement. The most important attempts were by the Council of the Southern Mountains, the Peoples Appalachia Research Collective, the Congress for Appalachian Development, the Highlander Research and Education Center, and the Appalachian Alliance.[11] These attempts to build a unified movement failed for a variety of reasons, but primarily because, unlike class, race, and gender, region in the United States does not provide an adequate political and economic focus for social movements.

This failure to create a social movement in Appalachia similar to the civil rights or women's movements does not mean that change efforts in the region have occurred in isolation. While many of these struggles have been local and concerned with a single issue, they have often been assisted by and associated with other groups and individuals within a loose alliance or network of Appalachian organizations. At times the network has had a name; at other times, it has been little more than an informal chain of individuals and groups. Organizations and activists come and go and financial support is rarely stable; but the network persists, and there may be no other like it in the United States.[12] Key players in this network today include the Highlander Research and Education Center, an adult education center in eastern Tennessee that has served as a meeting place, training center, and catalyst for social action throughout Appalachia and the South; the Southern Empowerment Project, an organizer training program established and controlled by grassroots community groups; and the Appalachian Community Fund, a community-controlled foundation that provides seed money and small grants to groups in the Appalachian region.

As Bill Horton points out, this loose, informal network "is the form that the Appalachian social movement has taken—slowly winning victories, working together, laying the groundwork, building or trying to build democratic organizations. Perhaps this is the way the movement will be built, piece by piece like a patchwork quilt until it comes together to rid the region of oppressive structures and practices, in turn becoming a piece of a much larger quilt that must be created to rid the nation of those same structures and practices."[13]

Over the past three decades, activists and academics have learned a number of important lessons about the politics of change in Appalachia. Successful change efforts in the Appalachian mountains have centered more often around the concept of community than around the centralized workplace of the mine, mill, or factory. In addition, historical memory and a reliance on and defense of traditional values—a strong commitment to land, kin, and religious beliefs, an emphasis on self-rule and social equality, and patriotism—have fueled many of the popular struggles in the region. Indeed, the fact that so many of the protests in Appalachia have been the result of defensive behavior—action to prevent the destruction of a way of life and a set of values that could be labeled traditional or conservative—has led one observer to refer to Appalachians as "reactionary rebels."[14]

While it is important to understand that grassroots resistance in Appalachian history has most frequently occurred in single-issue battles to preserve traditional values and ways of life, it is also necessary to recognize that there are limits to community-based organizing strategies that focus on single issues and rely heavily on localism and traditional values and institutions.[15] Community in our history entails exclusion as well as inclusion. Tradition and local values include racism, sexism, homophobia, and isolationism. In addition, while localism offers a number of advantages, few significant problems can be solved at the local level. Local resources have been depleted and local economies gutted by national and global market forces and the actions of the federal government and multinational corporations. Those organizing in Appalachia must find ways to make clear the connections that exist between local work and national and international institutions if local citizens are to understand the importance of national and international forces as determinants of what happens locally and to see themselves as actors at the national level.

Without attention to the larger questions of power in society, local community groups are often not prepared for the legal, political, and cultural forces that established powers bring against them. This results in a politics of gradualism—a strategy of adaptation and retrenchment—and a suspicion of outsiders and their programs. Further, it does not create the conditions necessary for coalition work with potential allies—be they health professionals, church workers, or environmentalists. Many local revolts throughout Appalachia turn out to be "flashes of independent anger" rather than sustained efforts at effective movement building precisely because they lack an analysis and understanding of power beyond the local levels.[16]

In sum, single-issue, defensive, localized work, which has characterized much of the organizing in Appalachia, can win occasional victories but cannot by itself lead to substantive change at an individual or structural level.[17] Tackling issues as complex as poverty, strip mining, or inadequate health care requires ongoing, multi-issue, reflective, democratic organizations, the type of organizing being conducted by SOCM, KFTC, and CFA—the multi-issue, membership-run organizations described above. These groups pursue an organizing approach that is flexible, pragmatic, and grounded in the past and present of members' lives. But unlike the narrow single-issue organizing of the past, these groups' primary concern is to empower their members for the long haul—to provide a schooling in politics and personal empowerment. They do so by offering a self-conscious leadership training program designed to develop democratic skills and build a sense of ownership and community. These organizations provide the space where participants can begin to see the connection between their concerns and those of other exploited people, where members can come to confront issues of racism and sexism, and where people can start to envision new alternatives to the world in which they live. As Connie White, a past SOCM president, puts it, "We don't care just about winning issues; we care more about helping people get stronger. In the long run, that is how you win issues and make real changes."[18]

In the past, many organizers have arrived in Appalachia with pejorative, romanticized, or contrived notions of the cultural forces and values present in the Appalachian mountains. Appalachian culture is "a web of both resistance and complicity,"[19] and it is important for those organizing in the region to develop an understanding of the ways in which regional culture informs the construction of class consciousness, race and gender relations, regional identity, and community life.

Several points need to be emphasized in this regard. First, regional identity and cultural pride are not naturally part of community life. Regional identity is not a geographical or cultural given in Appalachia, but must be understood as an outgrowth of political dynamics and social change. Similarly, local cultural traditions are selective and fluid in nature; they are "historically formed, situated, and altered by people interacting with each other and with social and economic forces."[20] These cultural traditions are at the heart of the community networks necessary to sustain people during protracted struggles and enable them to foster change on their own terms. But cultural expression does not always arise spontaneously in struggles to challenge oppression and inequality. The seeds for such expression exist; but these seeds must often be deliberately cultivated and nourished by organizers and institutions that recognize the value of cultural forms to resistance efforts.[21]

Second, neither class nor culture alone is a sufficient tool for understanding political action in Appalachia. Although classes are shaped by economic concerns, they are cultural configurations. Indeed, the United States is one of the few places where class and culture are thought of separately. Lived experience is different—our lives are a messy amalgam of identities out of which social relations are conducted.[22] The difficult but crucial task is not to decide between culture and class, but to discover how class, race, and gender conflicts express themselves today in cultural and political formations in Appalachia.

In Appalachian research, some of the most important work in this regard is being done by Mary Anglin and Sally Maggard. Using different approaches and studying protest in different locales and industries, Anglin and Maggard probe the ways in which gender, kinship, and social class interact to specify women's political experience, action, and consciousness. They demonstrate convincingly how and why change efforts, to be successful, must be situated in a web of work, family, and community needs and histories.[23] Other significant contributions include Michael Yarrow's investigation of the ways in which Appalachian coal miners' gender consciousness affects their class consciousness;[24] Richard Couto's discussion of community-based approaches to environmental risks;[25] and Dwight Billings's use of Antonio Gramsci's approach to religion to explain activism and quiescence among textile workers and coal miners.[26]

Third, racism is a major barrier to successful grassroots organizing and coalition-building in Appalachia, as it is throughout the nation. Don Manning-Miller charges that many of the community organizations in Appalachia, while committed either explicitly or implicitly to combating racism and to building a multiracial people's coalition for progressive social change, in practice pursue a process of organizing and struggle that fails to challenge the cultural conservatism and racism of their constituency. Manning-Miller urges organizers and activists to use all available media and organizational forms to confront people's racism and offers a number of valuable tactical measures and suggestions for developing a systematic program to confront racism in Appalachia.[27]

Finally, to be successful over the long haul, those engaged in cultural, educational, and political work must search through the regional culture to locate its most humane, progressive, and transformative elements and then look for ways to link these transformative elements to a larger human agenda for change.[28]

This brief consideration of organized grassroots change efforts in Appalachia should dispel the stereotypical notion of Appalachians as apathetic and dependent. Activists and scholars have made major advances since the 1960s in terms of building effective community organizations and in intellectual efforts to grapple with some of the tough issues involved in mounting effective resistance.

What is currently needed in the region is a critical discourse and practice "rooted in an awareness of popular traditions and resistance, but not blind to the wider contours of power within national and international capital." This requires a knowledge of a "people's" history and a history of capitalism.[29] It involves the creation of resistance organizations that take culture and community seriously as places for political action while encouraging their members to discover the ways their grievances are a result of "structural processes occurring at an economic, geographic, and political level far beyond the particular locale where the grievance is experienced."[30] It requires creating an alternative radicalism that chooses to complicate rather than simplify by incorporating themes from the many movements and traditions present in Appalachia and the United States.[31]

This critical discourse and practice require courage, commitment, struggle, and patience, and at times it is difficult to imagine that they are even possible. But occasionally an event occurs that helps us focus, that provides us with a glimpse of what could be. The United Mine Workers of America's occupation of the Moss 3 coal preparation plant during the 1989–90 Pittston strike was one such occasion.

The resistance leading up to the takeover was fueled by family, community, and union loyalties that had instilled in generation after generation a deeply felt class awareness and anger. Camp Solidarity, local community centers, and weekly rallies provided free spaces where striking miners, relatives, and supporters from all over the country shared life stories and experiences that reinforced bonds of community and class solidarity. Old labor and gospel songs rang out along the picket lines. American flags and yellow ribbons became the symbols of resistance to uncaring corporate and governmental leaders and structures. The miners and their supporters drew upon their religious beliefs to strengthen their resolve and justify their dissent. Strike leaders worked hard to educate the miners about the issues of the strike, to forge links with other social movements nationally and abroad, and to involve African Americans and women in a wide variety of strike activities. Mistakes were made, and much still remains unresolved. But for those few days those who were there were able to "feel the possibilities that reside within us, and in the groups of which we are or can be a part."[32]

www.ingramcontent.com/pod-product-compliance
Lightning Source LLC
Chambersburg PA
CBHW081423230426
43668CB00016B/2334